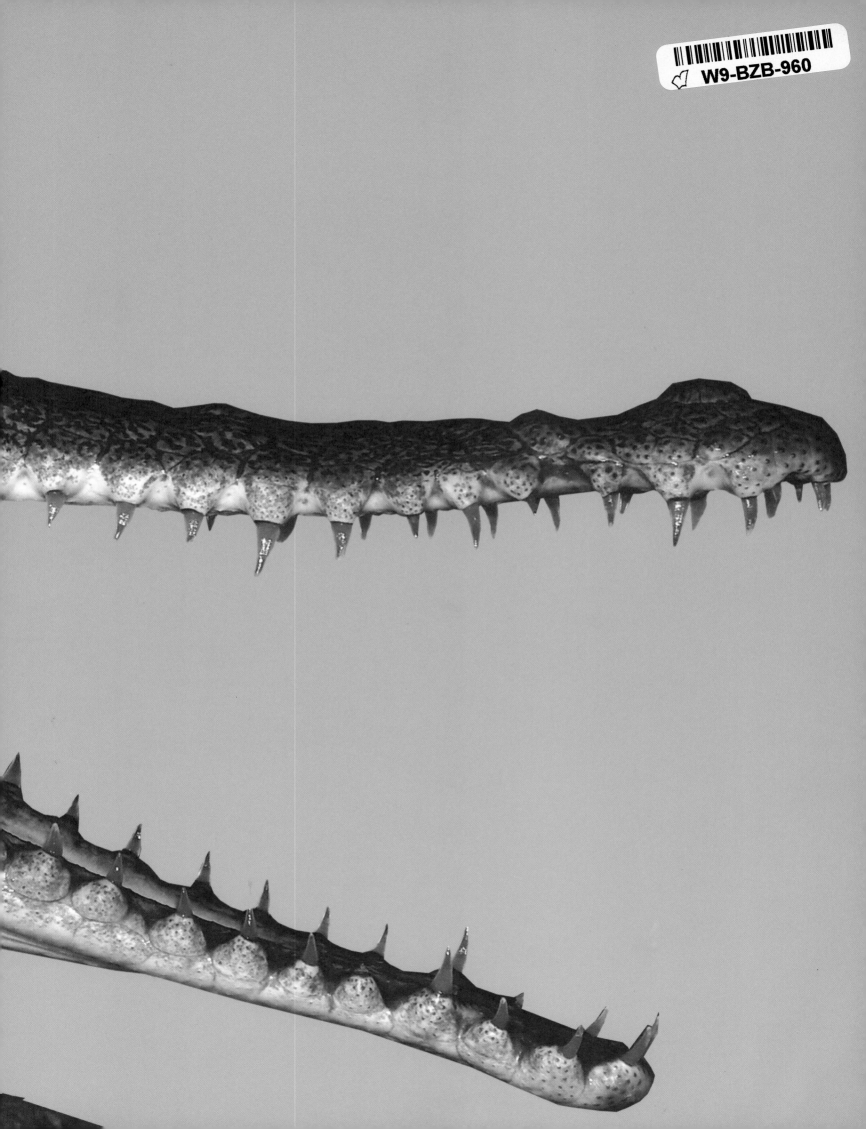

BIG BOOK OF ANIMALS

igloobooks

igloobooks

Written by Nathan Hamilton
and Deborah Chancellor

Photography: Ardea, Natural Visions,
istock.com, shutterstock.com, photos.com

Copyright © 2017 Igloo Books Ltd

An imprint of Igloo Books Group,
a Bonnier Publishing company
www.bonnierpublishing.com

Published in 2018
by Igloo Books Ltd, Cottage Farm
Sywell, NN6 0BJ
All rights reserved, including the right of reproduction
in whole or in part in any form.

Manufactured in China. LEO002 0918
10 9 8 7 6 5 4

Library of Congress Cataloging-in-Publication
Data is available upon request.

ISBN 978-1-78670-202-9
IglooBooks.com
www.bonnierpublishing.com

Contents

Worms

Any soft-bodied, legless animal with a length that exceeds its width is probably a worm. There are many different types. Most well-known are the earthworms, which are segmented worms, so called because their bodies are made up of different compartments, or segments. Other types of worm include parasites, such as nematodes, tapeworms and flukes, leeches and flatworms. Worms are found everywhere, even in the most inhospitable places on the planet.

▼ What is a flatworm?

Flatworms are the simplest type of worm and they have flat bodies that can be very thin. Many are parasites, like the dog tapeworm. This creature has a round head that attaches to the inside of a dog's intestines with sharp hooks. From here, it feeds on the partially digested food that passes through the gut from the dog's stomach. Sections of the worm drop off at its rear, carrying eggs outside the body. These eggs can infect another dog.

Where do you find Pompeii worms?

Pompeii worms are found very deep down in the Pacific Ocean in temperatures that are nearly hot enough to boil water. They cluster on the side of hydrothermal vent chimneys, close to where hot water and gases emerge from inside the Earth and spew into the sea. The temperatures here average 149°F (65°C), so Pompeii worms are the most heat-tolerant animals on Earth. These worms grow to about 4 in. (10 cm) in length.

When were Pompeii worms discovered? Only as recently as 1986.

Cat tapeworms have flat, ribbon-like bodies with up to 150 segments.

How do you tell male and female earthworms apart?

Both male and female organs are present in each individual, so you can't! Common earthworms are a type of segmented worm that are found all across the world. They do a vital job of breaking down waste materials and improving the soil. An earthworm's body is divided into about 150 ring-like segments and it breathes through its skin. They live in moist, rich soil at depths of about 1 ft. (30 cm). In the winter, earthworms dig deeper, away from frost, and lie coiled up in soil chambers.

Earthworms can consume up to one third of their own body weight in just one day.

Where do vent worms live?

Vent worms live deep under the Pacific Ocean, near where cracks in the Earth's surface cause temperatures to rise. Chemicals and molten substances from deep in the Earth's center form huge chimney-like structures, around which vent worms live. Vent worms feed with the help of billions of bacteria inside their red gills that convert harmful sulfurous chemicals collected from the vents into energy. These remarkable creatures can survive in sea temperatures of up to 131°F (55°C). They live in long white tubes, which may grow to about 10 ft. (3 m) long.

The vent worm, Riftia pachyptila, lives at depths of over 1 mi. (1.6 km) in the Pacific Ocean.

Slugs and Snails

Slugs and snails are a type of mollusk known as gastropods (which means "stomach foot") after their single, slimy suction-pad of a foot-muscle which they use to creep along. There are about 75,000 species of gastropods now known on land and in the sea, which makes them the largest class of mollusks. Slugs and snails eat plants and are considered pests as they devour crops and flowers. Their mouths are lined with rows of tiny teeth, that wear down one after the other.

▼ What is the largest land snail

The biggest land-dwelling snail in the world is the giant African snail. It can weigh more than 1 lb. 9 oz. (900g), which is nearly as much as a bag of sugar. Its body can reach 15 in. (39 cm) long and its shell alone can be as larg as 10 in. (27 cm) long. That's bigger than a soccer ball. It has been introduced from Africa into other warm countries as a pet, in zoos, or as a source of food. In many of these countries, it is now a pest as it has no natural predators.

Gastropods like the garden snail have a one-part shell, so they are called "univalves".

For farmers, the giant land snail is South East Asia's most destructive pest.

◄ How does the garden snail survive in dry weather?

The garden snail survives dry spells by finding as dark and damp a place as it can and then retreating far into its shell to preserve moisture. It leaves a layer of mucus around the edges of the outside that dries and sticks tight to the surface it is on. It also seals off the outside with dried mucus, leaving a "door". A snail's shell provides plenty of protection. Its vital organs are housed within it and the shell grows in a spiral as the snail grows. Like all mollusk shells, a snail's shell is made from a tough substance called calcium carbonate.

Why do slugs and snails leave a trail of slime?

Like all slugs and snails, the great black slug needs moisture to survive. It travels along the ground over a layer of slimy mucus. It is this mucus that causes its trail. To produce this mucus, its body needs to have a higher than average water content. The great black slug eats rotting vegetation and even the dead bodies of other slugs. It has a breathing hole behind its head on the right-hand side and, like other slugs and snails, it uses tentacles that can touch and smell to find food.

Like other gastropods, slugs lay eggs. When they hatch, baby slugs look like miniature adults.

How fast is a garden snail?
0.5 in. (1.3 cm) per second, at top speed. That's fast, for a snail.

Sea slugs are found mainly in the Red Sea and Indian and western Pacific Ocean.

How do sea slugs differ from land slugs?

Sea slugs belong to a completely different order of animals to slugs, called Nudibranchia. Instead of having a pair of lungs, like land slugs, sea slugs breathe through gills arranged in clumps on their backs that look a bit like plants. Like their land-dwelling relatives, they are slow moving and do not have shells. They have a nasty, poisonous taste and warn predators of this by being among the most brightly colored animals in the sea.

Squid and Octopuses

Squid, cuttlefish, and octopuses are specialized mollusks known as "cephalopods". They are the only invertebrates to have filled the same niche as fish. Unlike most other mollusks, octopuses and squid have no external shell. Squid have an internal shell and have 10 suckered legs. Octopuses have no shell at all and have 8 legs, or tentacles. Both have a beak-like mouth and highly developed senses, with sophisticated eyes that are similar to those belonging to mammals.

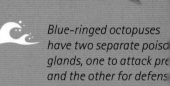

Blue-ringed octopuses have two separate poison glands, one to attack prey and the other for defense.

▼ How do reef squid move?

Like all cephalopods, the reef squid moves using jet propulsion. It sucks water in and jets it out again, propelling itself in the opposite direction. The Caribbean reef squid is often found in shallow reefs, and is not scared of divers. Their bodies are broad and less streamlined than many other squids, so they aren't quite as nimble. They are a mottled green-brown on one side with lighter coloring on the other as camouflage.

▲ Are blue-ringed octopuses dangerous?

They are very dangerous. They are the most deadly of all cephalopods to humans. The greater blue-ringed octopus carries enough venom to kill 26 adult humans in minutes and it is only about the size of a golf ball. This venom is more potent than any venom found in land animals. Luckily, they are not aggressive and will only sting in self-defense. Large shining blue rings cover its surface and they light up when it is alarmed.

How brainy is an octopus?

Cephalopods have the largest brains of all the invertebrates, and the common octopus has one of the largest brain-to-body size ratios, making it the cleverest known invertebrate. Scientists have conducted tests that prove its ability to learn complex signs to get food. Its brainy behavior in the wild includes using its tentacles to search crevices and rocks to find crabs and other small animals. It feeds by drawing food close with its suckered arms and biting its prey with its beak-like mouth.

Reef squid can communicate through changing the color of their skin.

No one has seen a giant squid in its natural habitat as it lives at such great depths.

Does anything eat giant squid?

Giant squid, and other deep sea squid, are a significant part of a sperm whale's diet. Dramatic underwater battles take place, and sperm whales may be permanently scarred by these encounters as the squid fights back and tries to escape. The giant squid can reach lengths of up to 59 ft. (18 m), and can weigh up to 1 ton (900 kg).

For how long does a blue-ringed octopus live? They don't live long, averaging just two years.

Common octopuses are usually solitary and defend their territories from others.

Crabs

Crabs are decapods, meaning they have 10 legs. As with lobsters, four pairs are for walking and one pair is for fighting, mating displays, and feeding. Like all arthropods, crab bodies are usually covered with a hard coating called an exo, or "outside", skeleton. A crab's abdomen is tucked away, giving them a rounder body shape. The abdomen is also narrower in males than in females. Crabs are omnivorous, and eat algae, worms, mollusks, bacteria, fungi, and carrion.

▲ Are pea crabs really the size of peas?

They certainly are, but they can grow as large as a fava bean. Pea crabs live in the shells of oysters, cockles, and mussels, moving in uninvited for protection. For this reason they are also called "oyster crabs", although they are found mainly in mussels. They can cause damage to the breathing apparatus of their hosts by occasionally taking a hungry nibble at their gills, and they also steal their host's food to survive. The pea crab is found from southern Scandinavia to western Africa, and throughout the Mediterranean.

▼ Where do hermit crabs get their shells?

Despite their name, hermit crabs aren't true crabs but are instead close relatives. They do not grow their own hard casings like other crabs, so they must use other empty shells, often mollusk or snail shells, and structures for protection, moving into larger shells as they grow. They move by dragging their shell along the ground with their legs and retreat into it when threatened.

Fully-grown female pea crabs can sometimes grow too large to escape the shells in which they live and are imprisoned for the rest of their lives.

Hermit crabs live in a variety of habitats. Some live on land, while others live in the sea.

The common shore crab is a very aggressive species, often fighting with its own kind.

Which crab lives in a rock pool?

Common shore crabs live in waters up to about 197 ft. (60 m) deep, but are often found in salt marshes, estuaries, and rock pools. Common shore crabs eat worms, small snails, other smaller crabs, algae, carrion or dead animals, mollusks, and whatever else they can find. It is more often young or immature common shore crabs that inhabit rock pools.

How much crab do humans eat?
Over 1.5 million tons a year.

How big is a Japanese spider crab?

Fully grown, the Japanese spider's leg span can be as large as 12 ft. (4 m), which is as long as a car, but it only weighs 42 lb. (29 kg). It is the largest of all the crabs. These spider crabs live at depths of up to 1000 ft. (350 m) at the bottom of the Pacific Ocean. Japanese spider crabs have orange bodies and their legs are thin with white spots. Despite its huge and fearsome appearance it is fairly docile. This makes them easy to catch and eat and they are under threat from humans.

The Japanese spider crab is a very old species of crab, and it is often referred to as a living fossil.

Centipedes and Millipedes

Centipedes and millipedes are arthropods with long, segmented bodies and many legs. Centipedes are predators that hunt using their claws and strong jaws that can inject poison into their prey. They are also flatter-bodied than the rounder-shaped millipedes. Millipedes are not predators but vegetarians, eating rotten or fresh plants. Each segment of a centipede has one pair of legs, while each segment of a millipede has two pairs. Millipedes therefore often have more legs than centipedes, but always less than the 1,000 in their name.

▼ How do millipedes defend themselves?

Although it is large, the giant millipede, like all millipedes, is quite slow and cannot bite or sting. So, a millipede's hard exoskeleton is the first method of defense: many smaller predators cannot pierce it with their jaws. Also, to protect their softer undersides, giant millipedes roll up into a ball and tuck in their legs. Some also secrete toxic substances from glands along the sides of their bodies or the middle of their backs. Some can even produce hydrogen cyanide gas.

The giant millipede coils tightly to defend itself from attack.

The giant centipede's body is made of between 20-23 segments and it has around 40-46 legs.

◀ Can centipedes really eat bats?

The giant centipede does. It is the largest centipede in the world and can grow longer than 12 in. (30 cm). To hunt bats, giant centipedes crawl into caves and dangle themselves from the ceiling. They then catch them as they fly by and disable them with their strong venom. They can also eat other larger animals such as lizards, frogs, birds, and mice. The giant centipede lives in South America and the Caribbean.

Millipedes have blunt heads to help them push through the leaf litter.

How do millipedes walk?

Millipedes walk by lifting each pair of legs at a time. It looks like they are moving along in a wave. Like centipedes, their eyesight is very poor and they sense their way by regularly tapping their antennae on the ground ahead of them. They have special hairs on the second or third pair of legs to keep the antennae clean. Millipedes are "detritivores", which means they eat rotting wood and leaves collected on the ground, and so play a part in nature's recycling process.

How many legs does a millipede have?
The largest number is 750, but most have between 80-400.

Centipedes can have as few as 30 legs, to as many as 170 legs.

Which centipedes live under rocks?

Common European centipedes are often found under rocks. They feed on insects, spiders, and other small invertebrates. An adult is about 1 in. (2.5 cm) long with around 30 legs. These centipedes' eyesight is poor, so they rely on their antennae to find their way around.

Cockroaches and Mantises

Cockroaches have flattened, oval-shaped bodies, chewing mouths, down-turned legs, and long antennae. Most species also have wings but often prefer to scuttle around on the ground. They are one of the most ancient insects on the planet and are great survivors. Slower-moving mantises are easily identified by their raised front legs, especially adapted for catching prey, and their compound eyes that are set high on either side of a highly maneuverable triangular-shaped head.

Do cockroaches stink?

Many do. Some species leave an unpleasant smell behind them after feeding. One, however, called the stinking cockroach, or the Florida woods roach, uses bad smells as a defense. When surprised or threatened, it releases a foul-smelling spray which can irritate human skin. It lives in central and southern Florida in the U.S.A. and lives in dead logs, tree stumps, and piles of firewood. When not defending itself from attackers, it actually smells like maraschino cherries.

How long have cockroaches been on Earth? For at least 340 million years.

The front legs of a praying mantis strike out in a fraction of a second.

▼ Do cockroaches live in families?

The young of many species of cockroach, such as the American cockroach, do stick together in family groups. It is because they eat wood. Wood is hard to digest, and cockroaches have a special type of microorganism that lives in their guts that helps them with breaking it down. Young cockroaches are born without this microorganism, however, and so must get their own. They usually do this by eating the skins and gut lining left behind by older cockroaches when they shed their casings. Adult cockroaches don't shed their skins, so newly-hatched cockroaches have to hang around their older brothers and sisters to pick up these digestive helpers.

Cockroaches can live for two to three weeks with no food and water, and up to 42 days without food.

How do mantises hunt?

Mantises are ambush predators, meaning they lie in wait for their prey and surprise it. Rather than lurking underneath a leaf or flower for their prey and striking upwards, which can be difficult and lead to mistakes, flower mantises improve their chances by actually sitting on the flowers themselves, taking advantage of their attractive properties for insects. This mantises has pink arms and a pink abdomen of an identical shade to the flower, and the thighs of its two back pairs of legs are expanded into pink petal shapes.

Mantises only have one ear and often cannot tell which direction a sound is coming from.

Do female praying mantises really eat their mates?

It's true that male praying mantises can risk being killed and eaten when they attempt to mate with females. They are smaller than the females, so they can be easily caught or wounded by their sharp front legs. Cannibalism isn't common and only happens when the female is hungry, and is probably due to mistaken identity. The male must always approach with caution, moving slowly while making the right signals with its antennae and legs.

Stick and Leaf Insects

Like mantises, stick and leaf insects often live in the branches of trees and bushes, and are exclusively vegetarian. They tend to be nocturnal feeders as they are slow movers and therefore vulnerable during the daytime. Because of this, many have developed very effective camouflage. Stick insects are "phasmids", which have elongated bodies that look like twigs or sticks. The main exceptions are the leaf insects that belong to the family "phylliidae" who have flattened bodies resembling leaves.

Swarms of stick insects can attract birds which gather to feast on them.

◀ Do stick insects live on their own?

Some species of stick insect can gather in very large numbers and cause quite a lot of damage. One species in Australia, "Didymuria violescens", can cause huge problems to eucalyptus trees. In 1963, a vast swarm of these stick insects stripped 650 sq. mi. (1,700 sq. km) of eucalyptus forest. That's the size of 240 soccer fields. Eucalyptus trees are not very resilient and can die if stripped of too many leaves.

Do stick insects have any other defenses?

Stick insects don't just rely on camouflage to protect themselves, some have other strategies. The New Guinean stick insect, "Eurycantha horrida", has sharp prickles all over its stout body and legs. If touched, it can use its back legs as a vice to crush its attacker. It can also curve its body around to make itself look like a snake about to attack. Other stick insects mimic scorpions about to strike and some can even spray chemicals backwards over a distance of 16 in. (40 cm) at predators.

There are about 2,500 different species of stick insect.

Can leaf insects fly?

As with many stick insects, the males can fly but the females are flightless. Green Javanese leaf insect females have large front wings that lie edge-to-edge on the abdomen. The way they are arranged looks like the vein system on a leaf. Like stick insects, female leaf insects don't always need a male to fertilize them and many let their eggs drop to the forest floor. In some species, eggs resemble seeds, and are collected by ants and housed in their nests.

Fossils of leaf insects have been found that are 47 million years old.

▼ How do stick insects hide themselves?

Stick insects don't always purposefully hide themselves in piles of twigs or undergrowth that looks like them. Instead, the intention of many is to resemble fallen twigs from the rainforest canopy high above. Such debris rains down almost constantly, and the lower leaves on rainforest trees catch them. A stick insect, like the bent twig stick insect, will often position itself in the middle of the lowest part of the leaf, where these falling twigs would normally rest. If disturbed, many species will simply fall to the floor like a stick to continue the disguise.

Most stick insects sway gently in the breeze to blend in with the rustling leaves around them.

Where do leaf insects live? They live in forests on islands in the South Pacific, Africa, Sri Lanka, and parts of northern Australia.

Flies

Although many bugs have "fly" as part of their name, flies are actually a completely separate group to other winged insects. The major difference is that they only have one pair of wings. In place of a second pair of hind wings, they have small body parts called "halteres" that help them balance when flying. As a result they are very skilled fliers. Nearly all flies feed by sucking up liquids like blood and nectar. Others have a kind of spongy organ that dissolves and absorbs their food.

▼ How do robber flies hunt?

Robber flies are fast fliers that attack and eat other flies and bugs. They have strong legs and can even catch their prey in midair. Like most flies, robber flies have two large compound eyes on either side of their head, but they also have three simple eyes in between these. Robber flies stab their prey with their short proboscis. They then inject a type of saliva containing neurotoxins into it. The toxins cause paralysis, and enzymes in the saliva digest the prey's insides.

Robber flies attack butterflies, moths, beetles, bees, dragonflies, grasshoppers, and even some spiders.

Housefly maggots can hatch in less than a day, between 8-20 hours after being laid.

▲ How do flies grow?

Flies undergo a complete metamorphosis, from a larval stage as a maggot into an adult fly after pupation, as do butterflies and many other bugs. A number of species eat rotting meat and dead flesh as maggots. Some types of maggots can also be used to treat a wound to prevent it from going bad, as they eat away all the infected flesh and leave the healthy flesh alone. Maggots are also a useful food for a number of different animals.

What do houseflies eat?

Houseflies eat anything sugary or rotting that they can dab up and absorb with their spongy mouthparts. The housefly is one of the most common insects and has followed humans wherever they have gone. This is because their behavior fits well with human activity. The flies lay their eggs in all sorts of animal manure and household waste. They are considered a pest as they can carry diseases in their saliva and on their bodies.

 Flies can beat their wings hundreds of times per second. Some species manage 1,000.

How long does it take for houseflies to grow from eggs? As little as 12-14 days.

Do all mosquitoes suck blood?

Mosquitoes' saliva contains an enzyme that prevents the blood from clotting.

Actually, male mosquitoes feed on the nectar of plants. Female mosquitoes are the ones that suck blood with their sharp mouthparts designed to pierce the skin. They need blood in order to make eggs. They are dangerous, however, because they can carry a number of unpleasant diseases, such as malaria, dengue fever, and yellow fever, and infect at the same time as they feed. Female mosquitoes lay their eggs on the surface of stagnant water and the larva that hatch feeds on animals and plant material before turning into a pupa in which it undergoes a full metamorphosis into an adult.

Butterflies and Moths

Butterflies and moths are different from other flying insects because they are covered in tiny scales. Although they look similar, there are easy ways to tell them apart. Butterflies fly during the day, whereas moths fly at night. Butterfly antennae end in club-like tips, while moth antennae come in a variety of different shapes, none of which end in a club. Butterflies rest with their wings raised while most moths rest with their wings laid flat.

▼ Do any butterflies migrate like birds?

Yes, monarch butterflies do. Each generation of monarch butterfly that hatches in Canada is able to find its way to Mexico to roost for the winter, at exactly the same place as generations before them. Scientists believe the monarch butterflies use the sun somehow as a compass to help guide them south. They believe that, as with most insect behavior, this information is stored in their genes. But, again, exactly how this works is not known. This is for a scientist in the future to solve.

The migration of monarch butterflies takes them over 2,000 mi. (3,200 km).

How fast can a death's-head hawkmoth fly? About 25 mph (40 kmph), but faster in short burs

Why are tiger moths so brightly colored?

Like many insects, tiger moths use their bright colors to warn predators of danger. These moths taste disgusting and can be slightly poisonous if eaten. Garden tiger moth caterpillars are also known as "wooly bears" as their bodies are covered with black hairs. These hairs help protect the young caterpillar, as predators find the furry coats hard to swallow.

Tiger moths can produce high-frequency sounds which jam the sonar system of bats.

The common yellow swallowtail has a wingspan of between 4-5 in. (8-10 cm).

◄ Why do swallowtail butterflies have long tails?

The common yellow swallowtail is widespread throughout Europe and can be found in mountain meadows in Austria, Italy, and Spain, as well as coastal areas and patches of wasteland. It gets its name from the shape of its wings, which resemble a swallow's tail. These are also a useful means of defense. It is not uncommon to find them with damaged tails. This is because birds and other predators are fooled into thinking the butterfly is the other way up, because the large red spots on its wings look like eyes and the tails look like antennae, giving the false impression of a head and allowing the butterfly vital moments to escape.

Male death's-head hawkmoths will run and hop around making high-pitched squeaking noises if disturbed.

▼ How do death's-head hawkmoths get their name?

Death's-head hawkmoths are named after the eerie skull-like pattern on their backs. Some people even believe that it's bad luck for a death's-head hawkmoth to come into your house. Unlike other moths that feed on flower nectar, death's-head hawkmoths ransack bee hives and nests for honey, earning them the nickname "bee tiger". Death's-head hawkmoths are strong fliers, spending the summer months in Europe and wintering in Africa. They lay their eggs on potato plants, and their numbers are declining because of insecticides used to protect the plants.

21

Bees and Wasps

Bees and wasps, along with ants, belong to a group called "Hymenoptera", which means "membrane wings". Bees and wasps both have four wings that are thin and see-through. They have small hooks joining the back of the front wing to the front of the back wing on each side, these are known as "married wings". Bees feed mainly on plants. They have long tongues that they can use to suck up the nectar from flowers. Wasps hunt other bugs, and some are parasitic.

▼ Do all wasps live in hives?

No, many wasps are solitary animals. Sand wasps make single nests in sandy soil. This takes a female most of one day to build. After inspecting the nest carefully, she goes hunting. Once she catches her caterpillar prey, she stings it several times and then drags or flies it back to the nest and lays eggs on it. When fully stocked with one or more caterpillars, the female seals the entrance with soil. When the eggs hatch, the young have a fresh supply of food.

 There are 20 species of sand wasp. Some build decoy nest holes to confuse predators.

▲ How do leafcutter bees build their nests?

Like most bees, the female leafcutter bee is solitary and builds individual nests. She does this by cutting an almost circular chunk from rose leaves. Then she carries the leaf segment back to a nest hole, often in a hollow plant stem or among the roots of cactus plants. She constructs a small chamber by sticking a number of leaf segments together, using their sticky sap. She stocks each chamber with nectar and pollen gathered from plants and then lays an egg on this food and seals the cell with more leaf fragments. The young leaf-cutter bee then has food when it hatches.

Do common wasps build nests?

es, common wasps build new nests every year. In spring, fertilized emales (or "queens") start building a new hive with paper made rom chewed-up wood. The queen then lays eggs on bits of hewed-up insects in sealed chambers. The eggs hatch and eat the ood and become "workers" that take over foraging for food and uilding the nest while the queen wasp lays more eggs. At the end f the year, new queens leave the nest with males to mate and then ibernate. Then they start the whole process again the next year.

How many trips to the hive does a honeybee make in a day? Each bee makes about 15 trips a day.

Common wasp nests can contain up to 10,000 individuals.

How do honeybees' hives survive in the winter?

Colonies of honeybees survive the winter because they generate warmth in the hive. They do this by contracting the muscles they use for flight but without flapping their wings, which looks like humans shivering. Honeybees need a lot of energy to do this, however, so the hive must be well stocked with honey. The honey is stored in hexagonal cells and sealed with bee's wax.

Bees visit hundreds of flowers each day, collecting pollen and fertilizing the plants.

Ants

Although ants are grouped with bees and wasps, there are a few differences. Ants usually have a more varied diet. Most ants are scavengers, searching the environment around them for whatever tidbits they come across. Others are purely vegetarian, and some are even aggressive predators that hunt other bugs. Ants are social animals, living in nests or large groups. Their nests can be made from a variety of materials, but ant nests can grow into much larger networks, housing many millions of individuals. Many ants have powerful stings.

Leafcutter ants' nests can be as much as 19 ft. (6 m) deep.

How large do ant nests grow? One colony of 45,000 connected nests in Japan contained 300 million individuals and 1 million queens.

▲ Why do leafcutter ants cut leaves?

Leafcutter ants live in the rainforests of Central and South America and build large nests underground in which they sleep at night. By day, however, they are hard-working farmers. Worker ants follow scent trails up to the tops of trees and cut pieces of leaf to carry back to the nest. Here, smaller worker ants chew the leaves into a sort of mushy compost on which they grow a fungus. The ants then "harvest" the fungus for food.

▼ Do all ants live in nests?

Unlike most ants, army ants don't build a permanent nest. Instead, they build temporary camps called bivouacs at the end of each day after searching for food in forests in Central or South America and Africa. Because of their numbers and their powerful jaws, they can kill and eat animals many times larger than themselves, such as mice and small birds. They form the walls of their bivouacs by clinging to each other with their legs.

An army ant colony may contain up to 500,000 individuals.

How do weaver ants make their nests?

Weaver ants live in tropical Africa, Australia, and South East Asia in nests built by pulling leaves together into small chambers. The ants work in teams, as they are not strong enough to move the leaves on their own. When a leaf is close enough together, the ants grab a baby ant, called a "grub", in their mouths, and push it over the leaf. The grub produces a type of silk that sticks the leaves together.

The difference in size between the smallest and largest weaver ant workers can be as much as tenfold.

▼ Why do wood ants farm aphids?

Wood ants protect aphids, mainly from ladybugs, by positioning themselves around them in trees and on plants while the aphids feed. This is in order to collect the drops of honeydew the aphids make while eating. Wood ants also feed on other small insects, using their strong bites to kill them and drag them back to the nest. They live in nests in the forests, and some gardens, of Europe.

The nests of wood ants can reach up to 6 ft. (2 m) high, that's about as tall as a large horse.

Ladybugs, Stags, and Titans

Beetles form the largest order of insects, with well over 350,000 known species. Along with butterflies, bees, and flies, they are considered to be one of the "more advanced" insects, because they undergo a complete transformation between their young, known as larva, and adult states. Winged beetles' soft hind wings fold under hard, protective front wings that meet and form a straight line down their backs. Their mouthparts are able to bite and chew, rather than being adapted for sucking like those of bugs. With tough, waterproof casings, beetles live all over the world and do many useful jobs.

Titan beetles are quite aggressive, but hiss a warning before attacking.

▼ How many spots does a ladybug have?

It depends on the species. Some have as many as 21 spots, others have none at all. There are over 3,400 species of ladybug all over the world, so there are all kinds of possible combinations of red and black, spots or no spots, some are even yellow. Their bold colors warn birds and other predators that these bugs taste bad. Ladybugs feed mainly on aphids, which are harmful to plants, making them very useful around the garden. They are found in meadows, gardens, parks, marshy places, and fields all over the world. Ladybugs gather in groups in winter and hibernate among leaf litter.

Ladybugs produce unpleasant chemicals from their knee joints to ward off predators.

▲ How big is a titan beetle?

The titan beetle can measure as large as 6 in. (15 cm) from the tip of its hard abdomen to the ends of its powerful jaws, or up to 8 in. (21 cm) if you include its antennae. It has been reported that it can snap a pencil in its mouth and that it can even cut into human flesh. These huge beetles are only found in and around the Amazonian rainforests in South America. Not much more is known about them, and scientists have yet to find any larvae.

Despite their ferocious appearance, male stag beetles are not aggressive and will only attack if threatened.

Why do dung beetles roll piles of poo?

Although it may seem odd to us, dung beetles are actually very fond of feces. They spend a lot of time skillfully constructing balls of dung to roll to a nest site so they, and their larvae, can eat it. In this way, these bugs are very useful recyclers, providing a welcome waste-disposal service for other animals. In some species, both the males and females cooperate in constructing one large dung ball. In other species, they might build one each. Many varieties are found rolling dung balls of various sizes in North America, Mexico, and Africa.

 In Australia, dung beetles were imported from Africa to help control flies by recycling the large amount of droppings from cattle.

How long do titan beetles live for?
No more than a few weeks in their adult state.

Why do stag beetles have such large jaws?

Male stag beetles have very large jaws. The mouthpart of the female is normally about one-sixth of her size. The males use their large jaws to fight over females and they do battle by trying to force each other off a tree trunk where a female might be likely to lay eggs. Male European stag beetles can measure up to 3 in. (7.5 cm) long and are found all over Europe. Worldwide, there are more than 1,000 varieties.

Spiders

There are close to 40,000 known species of spider and they have successfully occupied nearly every part of the world. All spiders have a pair of hollow fangs through which venom is released. Based on the arrangement of their jaws, spiders are separated into two groups: "mygalomorphs", that have jaws at the front of their head which strike downwards, and "true spiders", whose jaws are below the head and strike sideways in a pinching movement.

Trapdoor spiders drag their prey into their underground chambers to dine in peace.

Female black widows can produce 4-9 egg sacs every year, each containing about 100-400 eggs.

▲ Do all spiders make webs?

Not all spiders make webs, but all produce silk. Many hunt on the ground, like the jumping spiders, and some even build trapdoors. There are many different species of trapdoor spider. They build burrows in firm ground and many top them with a silk-hinged lid. Some species build a ring of trip-lines extending from the burrow. These spiders sit and wait, then rush out of their holes to catch passing prey detected through vibrations in the ground.

◀ Are black widows dangerous?

There are over 30 species of widow spiders, including the red back in Australia. Both the black widow and the red back are mainly black in color, with red on the underside or back of the abdomen to warn off predators. Eating a black widow or red back will normally not kill a predator, such as a spider-eating bird, but it would make it sick enough for them to learn to avoid it in future. They are quite dangerous to humans too. Most people recover from the bite after about a month, but five percent of those bitten die.

Which is the largest family of spiders?

The world's largest family of spiders is the jumping spider, with over 4,000 species. They are quite small, with large forward-facing eyes. These large eyes enable them to spot prey from a distance of over several inches, before stalking it and then leaping on top. Some can give painful bites, with reactions to venom lasting as long as two weeks, but none are fatal or dangerous to humans.

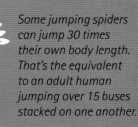

Some jumping spiders can jump 30 times their own body length. That's the equivalent to an adult human jumping over 15 buses stacked on one another.

Which are the largest spiders?

Tarantulas are the largest spiders in the world. Most live in silk-lined retreats on the ground, on cliff faces, or in trees. The largest species has a leg span of 10 in. (25 cm). Some tarantulas eat small vertebrates such as mice, birds, frogs, lizards, and snakes, even poisonous ones. They have clusters of hairs known as "brushes" on the ends of their legs that help them climb up smooth surfaces.

Is it true that all spiders have eight eyes?

Most do, but some only have six.

Tarantulas, like many spiders, cannot see much more than light, darkness, and movement.

Scorpions

Scorpions live all over the world but mostly occur in dry, warm regions. Like spiders, they have eight legs. Scorpions have a pair of venom glands located in the stinger, in the last segment of the tail, which they use mainly for hunting. Scorpion venom is designed to work best against other invertebrates, so most are not harmful to humans. They feed on a variety of insects, and the larger scorpions occasionally feed on vertebrates such as small lizards, snakes, and mice.

How do scorpions look after their young?

Unlike spiders, scorpions are born one by one, and the brood is carried on the mother's back until they are old enough to fend for themselves. This is after they have shed their first skin. Depending on the species, sometimes there can be as many as 100 young scorpions to take care of. The emperor scorpion takes especially good care of her babies, and does so for longer than most species.

The emperor scorpion can grow to 8 in. (20 cm) long and is one of the largest in the world.

How many species of scorpion are there? About 1,200 worldwide.

Are scorpions solitary creatures?

Most are, with one exception: the Arizona bark or crevice scorpion. Although it spends a lot of its time on its own, these scorpions gather in groups of up to 30 in winter to keep warm. They can normally be found scuttling around in rocky areas under boulders, logs, and tree bark. The bark scorpion is good at climbing and is sometimes spotted on the walls of houses in California, Nevada, South Utah, Arizona, and South Western New Mexico in the U.S.A. where it is the most common house scorpion.

▼ Do scorpions live in Europe?

The European yellow-tailed scorpion is found in warm European countries such as Italy or Portugal. It is quite small, growing to a maximum length of 2 in. (5 cm), and eats insects and other small invertebrates. It is expanding its range because of global warming, and colonies have now been found living in the United Kingdom.

The venom of the bark scorpion may cause severe pain and difficulty breathing, but human deaths are rare.

Yellow-tailed scorpions' venom is about as potent as a bee sting.

Which is the most venomous scorpion?

The deathstalker scorpion may be the most venomous. Its venom contains a powerful cocktail of a number of neurotoxins. In the wild, it lives in deserts and scrublands across North Africa and the Middle East. Compared to other scorpions it is fairly lightly built, with a long, thin tail, and quite narrow claws, probably because its powerful sting is defense enough. Another contender for the title is the fat-tailed scorpion of North Africa whose venom is similar to a cobra's in terms of toxicity.

Rays and Skates

Rays and skates are cartilaginous fish, this means their skeletons are made out of a tough, rubbery cartilage, instead of bone. Many of the 300 species of rays and skates live near the seabed, but some patrol nearer the surface. They have large wings on each side of their bodies, which they flap like a bird's wings to move through water. Their gill openings are behind their eyes on the top of their bodies, with their gills on their undersides.

Most manta rays have a wingspan of approximately 22 ft (7 m).

▲ Why do manta rays leap out of the water?

Manta rays are thought to leap out of the water to rid themselves of parasites, or to stun small fish by crashing down on top of them. It may be to escape predators or part of a courtship display. It could even be simply because they enjoy it. It is certainly spectacular: sometimes they even perform a full somersault. They are not dangerous animals, unless harpooned, when their thrashing, powerful bodies can be quite destructive. Manta rays usually travel alone, but have been observed swimming in pairs, or in groups of up to six individuals.

▼ Are stingrays dangerous?

They can be, with their long, spiny whipping tails. Normally they are not aggressive animals and they are unlikely to attack humans unless threatened. If they are pestered, caught, or stepped on, however, then their tails can whip out and sting with a venom that flows from the grooves in the side of their tail spikes. The rough tail stingray is one of the largest and it can reach up to 14 ft. (4 m) from front to tail tip and could deliver a nasty wound.

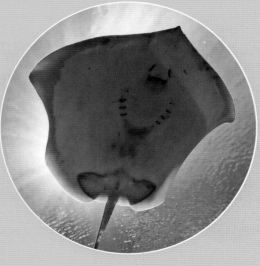

Most stingrays eat worms, crustaceans, or mollusks, but some attack larger fish.

What is an electric ray's shock for?

Electric rays are often quite slow moving, so their electrical charge can be used to stun quicker prey. It also serves as protection against predators, the shock would be enough to frighten away many, and is strong enough to stun a human. However, electric rays mainly eat worms, crustaceans, and other small animals that are slow moving, so it is thought that they may also use their electrical charge to help navigate.

What is a mermaid's purse?

Like many rays, skates, and sharks, the New Zealand rough skate lays an egg case that has coiled tendrils at each of its corners with which it can be anchored to rocks or plants at the bottom of the sea. The young take several months to hatch, and are vulnerable to predators during this time. When these egg cases wash up on the beach, they are known as a mermaid's purse.

Torpedo rays can generate 170-220 volts. That's nearly as much as the plug socket in a house.

How much does a manta ray weigh? The heaviest ever recorded was 3,000 lb. (1,400 kg).

The New Zealand rough skate grows to a length of up to 3 ft. (1 m).

Sharks

Like other cartilaginous fish, sharks have a rough skin, and they cannot fold their fins. Sharks have strong jaws and many have sharp teeth, but some have flat grinding teeth. Sharks have a highly developed sense of smell and can sniff out food from huge distances. There are around 400 species of shark, which includes some of the largest fish in the world.

Which is the fastest shark?

It is thought that the short-finned Mako shark is the fastest. This shark is well-adapted for speed and energy-efficiency. It is very streamlined and agile. It may manage bursts of speed up to 60 mph (95 kmph), but these estimates are thought to be a little high. Others put its top-speed at something closer to around 45 mph (70 kmph). It eats other fish such as tuna, which are also some of the fastest swimming fish.

The maximum known length of a great white shark is approximately 20 ft. (6 m).

How do great whites locate their prey?

At close range, the great white can detect the electrical currents generated by another animal's body. When further away, it has a powerful sense of smell that can track the scent of fish from a great distance. Great whites have good eyesight, with well-developed irises that can respond to light. They can see well in the dark and have a good sense of hearing.

What is the world's largest fish?

It's the whale shark, which lives in tropical and subtropical waters, often close to the coast. It feeds by swimming just below the surface with its huge mouth held open, gathering plankton that it can filter from the water with specially adapted gills. It sometimes eats assorted small fish, sardines, and even fish as large as mackerel can get swallowed up along the way.

 Whale sharks can grow over 42 ft. (13 m) in length.

How many people are killed by sharks? Shark attacks on humans are rare, and only between 6-10 attacks every year are fatal.

Why do hammerhead sharks have such unusual heads?

There is a lot of debate about why the hammerhead has an unusual shaped head. Having eyes on either side of such a wide "hammer" is thought to enhance the shark's vision and depth perception, allowing them a 360° view to spot prey above and below them.

 Hammerheads grow up to 14 ft. (4 m) long and are found in warm seas.

Bottom Dwellers

Bottom-dwelling fish spend their time feeding on the bottom of the ocean, in deep or shallow water. Many bury themselves or have flattened or camouflaged bodies, and their heads, mouths, and eyes may be strangely arranged to suit their different lifestyles. Some bottom dwellers feed off small organisms or plants, or the detritus of the ocean floor.

▼ Why do stonefish just lie around?

Lying still on the bottom of the sea is one of the best ways of conserving energy and many bottom-dwelling fish, like the stonefish, are very good at this. Most have developed camouflage as a protection, as otherwise they might be easy prey. The stonefish, however, goes one step further for protection and has extremely potent venom glands at the base of its strong spines. These are so sharp that they can even puncture the rubber sole of a shoe.

▼ Do stargazers really gaze at stars?

Not really, but they look like they do. Their eyes and mouths are both on the tops of their heads, which makes them look like they are gazing upwards. They are quite chunky-bodied and look a bit like toads. Like many bottom-dwelling fish, they bury themselves with only their eyes and mouths showing, some with a worm-like thread in their mouths with which to lure small fishes.

 Stonefish venom is fast-acting and is potentially fatal to humans.

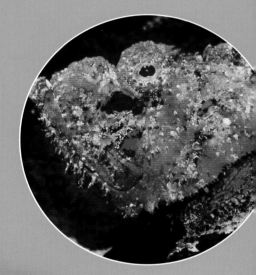

Stargazers can generate an electrical charge with special organs behind their eyes developed from the optic nerve.

Are there any bottom-dwelling sharks?

Many types of fish have bottom-dwelling counterparts. A shark called the monkfish, or angel shark, spends its life searching through the sandy bottom of the sea at depths of up to 330 ft. (100 m). Like many other bottom dwellers, it has a flat body and camouflage coloring or markings. Monkfish eat small seabed fish and detect prey using their electro-senses.

 Monkfish often partially bury themselves in sand.

How strong is the stargazer's electric shock? About 50 volts.

The peacock flounder's body can change to a lighter or darker shade, depending on its surroundings.

Why are flounders flat?

When flounders first hatch, they look like most other fish swimming in the water, but, before long, they start to lean to one side. Then the eye on the underside starts to move, until both eyes are on the "top". As the eye moves, the skull also twists round, with the mouth often ending up on top also. What is now the underside of the fish, then starts to lose its pigment and becomes white, as the topside darkens to blend in with the surrounding area.

Coral Reef Fish

Coral reefs are formed by the skeletons of corals. These reef-building corals live in colonies and bind together to form large structures. A coral reef is a thriving community for many species. Some coral like the shallower zones, others prefer the shelter of deeper regions. It is a complex system of inter-dependent relationships containing an amazing diversity of life.

▼ What is the biggest fish on the coral reef?

Giant groupers are the biggest bony fish that normally live on coral reefs. They can weigh as much as 900 lb. (400 kg), that's heavier than five men. Giant groupers eat lobsters, fish, and even small sharks, and often live in deep holes or caves. Because of their size, they are not very fearful of attacks and are generally slow-moving when not hunting. Their mouths are wide and their markings often blend with their surroundings.

Giant groupers can live for up to 40 years.

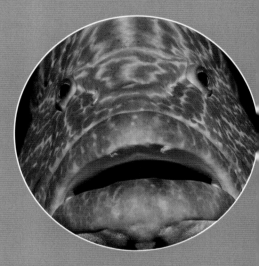

◀ Why do clownfish live in sea anemones?

Clownfish are a type of anemone fish that are often spotted in small groups living around sea anemones. Clownfish are immune to the venom in the sea anemones' stinging tentacles, so gain protection from larger predators. In return for this protection, clownfish clear the anemone of debris and chase away butterfly fish, which eat its tentacles.

Clownfish are quite bold for their size and will chase away much larger fish, especially when guarding eggs.

How do queen angelfish defend themselves?

The queen angelfish is probably one of the prettiest fish on the coral reef and has some interesting markings. It is named "queen" because of a spot on the top of its head, that some think looks a bit like a crown. It also has a spot on its front fins and mouth. These spots are like false eyes, and confuse predators over the fish's direction of movement, size, and the possible location of vital areas such as the head, eyes, and gills.

 Most angelfish are solitary and swim constantly, often on a set route.

Why are lionfish striped?

Lionfish are also known as scorpionfish, and are often quite boldly colored. As elsewhere in nature, these bright stripes of color may warn of potential danger to attackers. However, even when on a crowded and colorful coral reef, its typical red, brown, and white bands blend in with its surroundings. Some species have grooved venom spines located on their head and in their fins, and the stings can cause severe pain to humans.

Why do clownfish not get stung? Their bodies are protected by a coating of mucus.

A lionfish's spines act like hypodermic needles, injecting poison from glands at their base.

Freshwater Fish

Freshwater fish live in streams, rivers, lakes, or canals rather than the open sea. Freshwater only makes up about 2-3 percent of all the world's water, mostly in the polar ice caps, and less than one percent of the Earth's surface, and yet it contains a huge variety of species. These habitats are at risk due to human activity and pollution.

Species of Siamese fighting fish have been selectively bred as pets, and some even have fins longer than their bodies.

▼ How do jewel cichlids care for their young?

The jewel cichlid is normally a quarrelsome, aggressive fish that is very territorial. However, these animals mate for life and have a highly developed sense of brood care, giving their young a better chance of survival. After the eggs have been laid and fertilized, the adult pair guard the nest. One will fan water over the eggs, while the other stands guard. Even as young fish, the parents continue to care for them, protecting them from predators.

▼ When do piranhas eat larger prey?

Red piranhas are perhaps one of the most famous carnivorous freshwater fish. Usually, these predators feed on other, smaller fishes, but they can also eat much larger prey. This is usually only as a result of a chance encounter with a wounded animal. A sudden strong smell of blood can send piranhas into a frenzy searching for the source. When they find it, a large school of piranhas can strip an animal to bare bones within minutes. Each fish makes repeated, lightening strikes with its razor-sharp teeth.

Piranhas are mainly found in South America, where locals have used their sharp teeth as weapons.

Normally a slightly duller color, jewel cichlids change to bright red at mating time.

How do Siamese fighting fish fight?

The dramatically colored and large-finned male Siamese fighting fish are very territorial and will fight bitterly if one invades the other's space. To start with, they spread out their fins in a display of aggression to deter rivals. If this doesn't work, they will then lunge for each other, biting and tearing at the others' fins. Eventually, one will give up and leave.

What is the largest freshwater fish? The Mekong giant catfish.

The pike is Britain's largest freshwater fish and can reach 5 ft. (1.5 m) in length.

▶ How do pikes hunt?

Like many carnivorous fish, the pike is an ambush predator that lies in wait for its prey and then strikes suddenly. Pikes are solitary predators that hide in reeds or behind rocks. When prey approaches, the fish rushes out, aided by its slim, streamlined, elongated body. Larger pike have even been known to hunt ducklings and young coots from the surface of lakes. They have strong, beak-like jaws and sharp teeth.

Hunting Fish

Blue marlin and sailfish are known as "billfish" because of their large bills, which are long and rounded. The swordfish is slightly different and has a longer, flatter bill, and so is grouped separately. All three of these fish are very muscular and fast, and the marlin and sailfish are known to leap out of the water. The barracuda is another unrelated hunting fish and has an elongated body and strong jaws with sharp, fang-like teeth. All these fish are found in tropical and subtropical oceans.

 Barracudas have forked tails, large eyes, and dark blotches on a background of silvery scales.

▶ How do marlins swim?

Like the swordfish and sailfish, marlin have two ways of swimming that use two different sets of muscle, one fast and one slow. One is for when they are cruising and conserving energy on longer trips and the other is for shorter bursts of high speed, which can be up to 50 mph (80 kmph). Although not usually dangerous to humans, marlins have sometimes leapt out of the water and speared unlucky fishermen trying to catch them.

 Because they are so fast and strong, the blue marlin and sailfish are prized catches for human fishermen.

How do barracudas hunt?

Barracudas are curious fish that are attracted mainly to shiny, flashing objects that look like fish scales. It is therefore thought that they hunt using sight more than smell. Barracudas are often solitary predators but younger fish congregate in sandbar and can hunt in packs. They eat all kinds of smaller fish and sometimes herd them together when they are full, waiting until they are hungry enough for another meal.

▼ How fast is a sailfish?

Sailfish are the fastest fish in the sea, reaching speeds of nearly 70 mph (110 kmph). Sailfish have extremely streamlined bodies and huge sail fins which are folded back when swimming, but raised when it feels threatened. They reach lengths of 11 ft. (3.5 m) and their bodies are packed tight with muscles. They can swipe their tails quickly to generate bursts of speed.

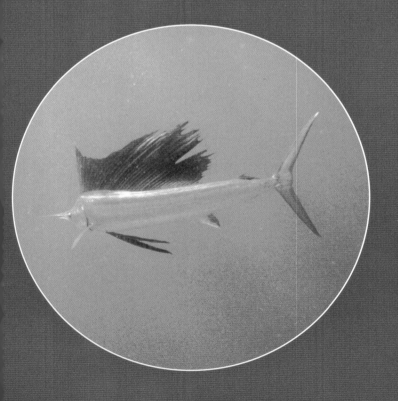

▲ How is a swordfish different from a marlin?

Swordfish have longer bills or "swords" than the marlin, which can account for up to 30 percent of their overall body length. They also lose their teeth and scales as they grow older and they lack the longer, strap-like ventral fins of the sailfish or marlin. They hunt using their bills to slash at, injure, and stun their food, which they then swallow. Swordfish can weigh as much as 1,200 lb. (550 kg).

 A swordfish's sword is made of bone covered by tough skin.

Sailfish eat fish and squid, chasing them at high speeds through the water.

Newts and Salamanders

Newts and salamanders are amphibians that look like lizards, but they do not have scales. They are usually active at night and they have long, slender bodies and quite short limbs, but with long tails. In total, there are over 450 species, but this is likely to increase as more continue to be found. Some species can climb trees, but most hide under rocks or logs until darkness or wet weather arrives. They often lay their eggs in water, but many salamanders lay their eggs on land.

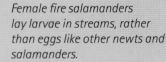

Female fire salamanders lay larvae in streams, rather than eggs like other newts and salamanders.

▼ How do Japanese fire-bellied newts swim?

Japanese fire-bellied newts use their long, flattened slender tails by wriggling them from side to side. It is a species that spends most of its life in water and is a fast and agile swimmer. Like many newts and salamanders, its bright coloring warns that it can produce toxins that are harmful or that taste unpleasant. Mating pairs go through a long courtship of water dances during which the male fans and beats his tail rapidly at the female.

Japanese fire-bellied newts are often active during the day.

▲ How do fire salamanders protect themselves?

Fire salamanders have two rows of enlarged glands, called paratoid glands, running along the middle of their backs from which they are able to spray toxic secretions. They can direct these sprays quite accurately over distances of nearly 6.5 ft. (2 m). These toxins can affect the central nervous systems of their predators and cause eyes and mouths to itch. After their larval stage, fire salamanders spend nearly all their lives on land.

How much time does an adult newt spend in the water? Anywhere between 1-210 days a year.

The red-bellied newt contains enough toxins to kill a man, so it warns predators not to eat it.

Olms can reach a length of 1 ft. (30 cm).

▲ What is an olm?

An olm is a species of salamander that never really seems to grow up. Instead, they keep many of their larval features for life. Adult salamanders can breathe through their skin and can also breathe through lungs. The olms, however, keep the gills that salamanders have as larvae and never shed them. They are also faded in color, often in washed out grays, pinks, or yellows. They have very small eyes but large tails to help them swim.

Why does the red-bellied newt curl itself into a circle?

When the red-bellied newt curls itself up it is performing an unusual behavior pattern known as the "unken" reflex. This is named after the fire-bellied toad, called "unke" in German, which also behaves this way. When threatened, the red-bellied newt shuts its eyes, stretches out its legs, and bends its head and tail back over its body. This is in order to display as much of the colorful parts of its body as possible. This warns the predator that it tastes bad to eat.

Frogs

Frogs are amphibians with long back legs for jumping. Their anklebones are stretched, which gives them extra leverage when leaping. Frogs differ from toads in that they usually have smooth, shiny skin while toads have duller, warty skin. Frogs are found in humid, hard to reach places such as rainforests. We have much to discover about them, and new species are still being identified. The most familiar frogs are those that produce spawn in ponds, which hatch into tadpole larvae and then grow into adult frogs.

The nest-building gray frogs live in Southern Africa and, like most frogs, eat insects.

▼ Which is the most poisonous frog?

The golden poison dart frog of South America is the most poisonous frog. It comes in a variety of bright colors, such as mint green, yellow, and orange, each one warning of the nasty surprise it holds for any animal wanting to eat it. It is so poisonous that it is unsafe to handle. The poison dart frogs take their name from the practice of native South American hunters who use the secretions from the skin of these frogs to poison their hunting darts.

▲ Do frogs build nests?

To protect their vulnerable eggs from predators, African gray tree frogs lay their eggs in a foam nest attached to a branch above water. The female produces eggs along with a liquid. Then the male, who holds onto the female during mating, beats this liquid into froth. As the froth hardens, it protects the eggs, creating the nest. A number of different mating pairs may work together on one large, communal nest. These nests are made in trees overhanging water so that when young tadpoles hatch, they drop into the pool.

A dart made from the secretions of a poison dart frog can remain deadly for up to one year.

Which toad looks dead?

The Surinam toad is actually a species of frog that looks as if it has been flattened. As well as being one of the most bizarre-looking of all frogs, it has a strange way of breeding. As the female lays her eggs, the male fertilizes them and places them onto her back, pressing them down with his belly. Over a few days, they sink further into her squishy skin. In some species, they hatch as tadpoles from her back.

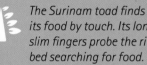

The Surinam toad finds its food by touch. Its long, slim fingers probe the river bed searching for food.

How many species of frog are there?
Over 4,750 and more are being found all the time.

▶ Why do Darwin's frogs swallow their young?

They don't but it looks like they do. Female Darwin's frogs lay their eggs on land. Males then gather and wait around eggs that are ready to hatch and gobble up the small tadpoles into their mouths as they emerge. They do not swallow them, however. Instead, the male of one species, Rhinoderma darwinii, hides the tadpoles away in his vocal sac until they are ready to emerge as small frogs. Another similar species, Rhinoderma rufum, carries the tadpoles to water.

Male Darwin's frogs can carry up to 15 tadpoles in their vocal sacs.

Toads

Toads are generally heavier-set than frogs, with shorter legs and more warty-looking skin. They have a large bump behind their eyes known as a paratoid gland. Toads are usually ground-dwelling and typically hide in holes during the day, emerging at night to look for food or to mate. Like frogs, they lay eggs that hatch into tadpoles. Many species of toad hunt insects, flicking out their sticky tongues to catch them. Other species ambush their food.

The last sighting of a golden toad was in 1989. In 2004, the IUCN declared the species extinct.

▲ Which are the most colorful toads?

The golden toad lived in the rainforests of Costa Rica. They spend most of their lives hidden in holes dug into the extensive root systems of forest trees. They emerge for a few days each year in order to mate in small pools and streams. Male golden toads are a golden orange in color and the females are deep red with large brown blotches. They are one of the most colorful of all toads.

◄ What do cane toads eat?

The cane toad is a very hungry predator indeed. It eats almost anything it can get inside its large mouth including birds, mice, and fish, along with the usual insects, slugs, and earthworms. Cane toads are native to Texas and South America, but they have been introduced into other areas for pest control. Unfortunately, because of their voracious appetites, such introductions have usually had disastrous results for other local frog or useful insect populations.

The cane toad can grow up to 10 in. (24 cm) long, and can weigh 5 lb. (2.6 kg).

Do toads give you warts?

There is no evidence to prove that toads give people warts, but it's not a good idea to pick them up. All toads produce secretions and unpleasant toxins, of varying strengths, to repel predators such as birds, foxes, and other animals. Their warts are enlarged skin glands designed to excrete these defenses. A number can be quite dangerous. The Colorado river toad's toxin, for example, can produce powerful hallucinogenic effects in humans if eaten.

Colorado river toads live in the southwestern United States and eat small rodents and insects.

How many eggs can a toad lay? As many as 20,000.

Common toads wait for rainy weather before leaving the pond in which they were born.

Which toad hunts bees?

The European common toad has been seen sitting outside beehives in early evening, waiting to catch the bees as they return. They are known to hunt any small, dark colored moving object it may encounter at night, such as flies, worms, caterpillars, and even small mice. European common toads are quite stocky in appearance and the females can grow up to 7 in. (18 cm) in size, which is around the same size as a man's hand.

Tortoises and Turtles

Turtles and their close relatives, tortoises and terrapins, are among some of the world's oldest reptiles. Giant turtles were swimming in the sea when dinosaurs were roaming on the land, over 65 million years ago. Today, there are about 240 different kinds of turtles, tortoises, and terrapins. Tortoises live on dry land, terrapins swim in freshwater rivers and lakes, and turtles live in the oceans.

The biggest leatherback turtles can grow up to 8 ft. (2.4 m) long, which is about the length of a rowing boat. They can weigh up to 2,000 lb. (900 kg), which is about ten times heavier than an average man.

▼ How big are terrapins?

Terrapins are smaller than turtles. The red-eared terrapin of North and South America grows to just 10 in. (25 cm) long. It eats fish, insects, and freshwater plants. The red-eared terrapin is a sociable animal, living in large groups. It is active by day, and likes to spend time out of the water sunbathing on riverside roots or floating logs. Female terrapins lay clutches of up to 22 eggs, which hatch after about three months.

▲ Where do leatherback turtles live?

Leatherback turtles swim in warm seas around the world. Like all turtles, they spend their whole lives at sea. Female turtles come onto land when it is time to lay their eggs. Amazingly, they always come back to the beach where they hatched to do this. When a female turtle has laid her eggs, she covers them with sand and returns to the ocean. Her parenting job is complete. The sun warms the eggs until they hatch.

Do tortoises, turtles, and terrapins have teeth?
No. They cut and tear their food with their sharp, beak-like jaws.

The shell of a tortoise, terrapin, or turtle is made up of about 60 hard, bony plates, which cover the animal's back and underbelly. Only the head, tail, and legs stick out from this protective armor.

A tortoise protects itself by drawing its head, legs, and tail up inside its shell. It is very hard for a predator to beat this defense tactic.

▼ How do turtles breathe?

Turtles breathe air, just like land tortoises, but they can hold their breath underwater for up to two hours when they are resting. When sea turtles are active, they have to return to the surface to breathe every few minutes.

Where do Galapagos tortoises live?

Galapagos tortoises live on the Galapagos Islands, which are off the coast of Ecuador in the East Pacific Ocean. They grow up to 5 ft. (1.5 m) long, and the males are usually bigger than the females. Large land tortoises such as the Galapagos tortoise grow very slowly. They can live for well over 100 years, which is longer than most other kinds of animals and humans.

Hawksbill turtles swim in the Atlantic and Pacific Oceans, and stay fairly close to the shore. Hawksbills feed on sea grass and small marine animals.

Pythons and Boas

All snakes are meat-eaters, but they kill their prey in a number of different ways. Constrictors do not use poison, but squeeze their prey to death. Boas and pythons are closely related to each other, and are both in the constrictor family of snakes. They coil themselves around their victims, squeezing more tightly each time the prey breathes out. Once the prey is dead, the snake swallows it whole.

Pythons open their jaws wide to eat their prey. When a python swallows a very large animal, its ribs expand to fit the prey inside its body.

▼ Where do green tree pythons live?

Green tree pythons live in the rainforests of New Guinea. They look like the emerald tree boas of South America, and behave in the same way. Both types of snake sleep in trees during the day, and hunt for prey at night. Their green skin keeps them well hidden in their leafy habitat. Adult green tree pythons are green but, when they first hatch out of their eggs, they are a bright yellow, and sometimes even red. After about a year they change color.

▲ Where do carpet pythons live?

Carpet pythons live in a variety of habitats in Australia. They are very adaptable, equally suited to life in the rainforest and in the desert. The carpet python preys on many different animals, including small marsupials, rodents, and lizards. Carpet pythons have an interesting pattern on their scaly skin, which looks like the design on an oriental carpet. This elaborate pattern provides good camouflage as the python lies in the shadows, waiting for its prey to pass by.

All snakes have long, scaly bodies, and slither about on their bellies as they have no legs. They are cold-blooded reptiles, which means they have to rely on the temperature of their surroundings to control their body heat.

Common boas grow up to 12 ft. (3 m) long. Like all snakes, they never stop growing, and shed their skin regularly.

How many species of snake are there?
There are 3,000 species.

▼ Which is the world's heaviest snake?

The green anaconda of the South American rainforest is the heaviest snake in the world. This massive 29 ft. (9 m) long constrictor weighs about 500 lb. (227 kg). That's about 7 times heavier than the average eleven-year-old child. The green anaconda can crush a caiman to death, then swallow it whole. It weighs more just after a meal like this. Green anacondas are also known as "water boas", as they spend much of their time near rivers. After a meal, an anaconda will bask in the sun while it digests its food.

Are common boas dangerous?

Common boas are also known as boa constrictors. They are not thought to be a danger to humans, but they have been known to hunt and eat animals of all sizes, from birds and monkeys, to wild pigs. Boa constrictors are found throughout Central and South America, from Mexico to Argentina. They live in deserts, rainforests, grasslands, and farmland.

Green anacondas can move faster in water than on land. They are good swimmers, and spend a lot of time in the rivers of the South American rainforest.

Venomous Snakes

About one-third of all species of snakes use poison to kill their prey. Many kinds of snake, including cobras and boomslangs, inject venom into their prey though sharp fangs. This venom is a neurotoxin which paralyzes the victim, so it can't fight or run away from the snake. Other snakes, including vipers, use a kind of poison that eats away at the flesh of its prey.

▼ Why do rattlesnakes rattle?

Rattlesnakes are named after the rattle on their tail, which they shake to warn off predators. A rattlesnake's poison is in its mouth, not in its tail. The most deadly rattlesnake in North America is the Mojave rattlesnake. One bite from this snake contains enough poison to kill 15,000 mice. The eastern diamond-back rattlesnake is the biggest species of rattlesnake. At 8 ft. (2.5 m) long, it is about the length of a motorbike. When rattlesnakes shed their skin, they leave behind old scales on the tip of their tails. These dead scales rub together to make a rattling noise. The older a rattlesnake is, the louder its rattle.

 Rattlesnakes are vipers. All vipers have fangs at the front of their mouths, which inject poison into prey. The fangs fold back into its jaws, so the snake can shut its mouth.

▼ Can snakes swim?

Many snakes are excellent swimmers, taking to the water to escape from predators or to cool off. Some species of snake actually live in the sea. There are over 50 species of sea snake, and some of them are extremely poisonous. Sea snakes do not have gills like fish, so they can't breathe underwater. They can hold their breath for at least an hour at a time, but then they have to come up to the surface for some air. Sea snakes shed their skin more often than land snakes, about once every other week.

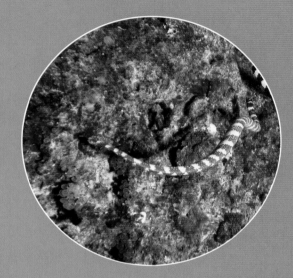

 Sea snakes swim in the warm waters of the south and western Pacific Ocean. Many have very strong venom in their hollow fangs, so they can over power their prey before it swims away.

Does a snake's poison kill everything? No, the poison usually works best on the animals it eats, while other animals may be immune.

When agitated, the Cape cobra rears up and flattens
it neck so that its hood can be seen clearly. It hisses its
warning, but this aggressive snake is quick to strike.
Cape cobra venom causes respiratory failure in its prey.

Boomslangs can be dangerous, but they are
only aggressive towards humans if they
are frightened. A boomslang puffs up its
throat as a warning if it is threatened.

What are boomslangs?

oomslangs belong to the Colubridae snake family.
ll Colubrids have teeth, but only a small number
ave rear fangs. Three quarters of all snakes are
olubrids, most of which are harmless, but
oomslangs' venom is very toxic. Like all snakes,
oomslangs have very sharp senses, which help them
o detect their prey. Boomslangs have large eyes,
o they can see well in their African forest homes.
hey lunge at prey, such as birds, lizards, and frogs,
alf swallowing it before delivering a deadly bite.

Why do
cobras stand up?

Cobras are poisonous snakes that live in
Asia and Africa. When they are threatened,
they rise up from the ground and open out
their hoods to frighten predators away.
Some cobras, such as the Indian cobra,
have hood markings that look like
eyes. This confuses an attacker,
giving the snake a chance
to escape.

Crocodiles and Alligators

Crocodiles and alligators belong to a group of reptiles called the crocodilians. These fierce carnivores have not changed much for millions of years, since they hunted in prehistoric swamps while the dinosaurs walked the Earth. Today, there are 14 species of crocodile, two species of alligator and six species of caiman. There is just one more species, the Indian gharial, which looks different from the others, with a long, slender snout.

The eyes and nostrils of all crocodilians are high on their heads, so they can see and breathe while most of their bodies are underwater.

When baby crocodiles hatch out of their eggs, they call out for their mother. Just like a newborn human baby, a baby crocodile needs to make a noise to get attention.

▶ How do crocodiles care for their young?

Crocodiles make much better parents than many other reptiles. A female Nile crocodile lays up to 75 eggs, burying them under sand in the riverbank. She guards them for about three months until they hatch, then carries them gently in her big mouth down to the water. She goes on protecting them from predators for another few weeks, before leaving them to fight their own battles. Crocodiles devour small prey whole, but they rip up the flesh of larger prey, such as deer, before they eat it. They can't chew their food so they swallow stones, which grind their food inside their bellies, mashing it into a pulp. They do not need to eat often, only having a big meal about once a week.

▲ What do caimans eat?

Caimans look like alligators, but they are smaller, with shorter snouts. However, their jaws are still wide enough to be able to hunt a variety of prey, such as fish, birds, lizards, and small mammals. They usually hunt at night, swallowing their prey whole in the dark. Many caimans live in the warm, tropical rivers of Central and South America. Some are found on islands in the Caribbean. Caribbean caimans' ancestors probably swam there, or drifted on ocean currents, from the South American mainland.

Where does the gharial like to hunt?

The gharial hunts in fast-flowing rivers, where there are plenty of fish to catch in its long, thin jaws. This specialized fish hunter is found in India and Pakistan, swimming in large rivers, such as the Ganges and the Indus. Unlike its bulkier crocodilian relatives, the gharial has weak legs and can't walk well or easily on land. It spends nearly all its life in the water, but will haul itself onto the riverbank to rest and bask in the sun.

Crocodiles and alligators have thick, scaly skin, which is an effective defense against attack.

Which crocodile is the biggest? The saltwater crocodile is. It grows up to 20 ft. (6 m) long. That's about twice as long as a speedboat.

▼ How fast are alligators?

Alligators, such as the American alligator, can run fast on land, but they are even quicker in the water. To swim, they tuck their legs under their bodies and swish their strong tails from side to side.

The American alligator lives in southeastern U.S.A. in warm rivers and swamps. It will eat almost anything it can catch, including water birds, fish, and turtles. In populated areas, the American alligator will sometimes ambush farm animals that have strayed too close to the water.

You can tell alligators and crocodiles apart by their teeth. When an alligator shuts its mouth, you can't see any teeth in its bottom jaw. When a crocodile has its mouth closed, you can see the fourth tooth on each side of its bottom jaw.

Flightless Birds

Of the roughly 10,000 species of bird, around 40 are flightless. It is thought that flightless birds are all descended from birds that could fly at one time or another, and that they have lost the ability over time. This could be due to changes in habitat, lack of natural predators, or a specialization in other forms of travel, such as fast running or skillful swimming.

▼ Why can't an ostrich fly?

In short, because it is too big! The ostrich is the biggest bird on the planet. It reaches 9 ft. (2.5 m) in height and weighs about 320 lb. (145 kg). Scientists have calculated that no bird over about 40 lb. (18 kg) would be able to fly, because their muscle power could never be enough to get them airborne. Ostriches are fast runners, reaching speeds of up to 45 mph (70 kmph).

▼ How does a little spotted kiwi find food?

Like other kiwis, the little spotted kiwi of New Zealand finds its prey by smell, using nostrils on the end of its beak. Its food includes small insects, and worms. Like many other flightless birds, the kiwi is threatened with extinction because of the introduction of predators such as domestic cats and pigs.

Male ostriches are black with white feathers, whereas females are gray-brown.

Although small, the little spotted kiwi lays the largest egg for its body size, at a quarter of an adult's weight.

◀ How deep can an emperor penguin dive?

Although they are a little unsteady on land, emperor penguins are expert swimmers and can dive to depths of up to 820 ft. (250 m) searching for fish. They are also capable of huge feats of endurance. Over three winter months in the Antarctic, one of the coldest places on earth, the male emperor penguin shelters his egg on his feet, protecting it from the ice.

 The emperor is the world's largest penguin and stands at up to 4 ft. (1.2 m) high, which is about the height of a six-year-old child.

Where does the emu live?

Where does the emu live? The emu lives in Australia and is the second largest bird in the world. Emu eggs are a dark green color when they are first laid, but darken to a glossy black within a few days. A female can lay up to 10 eggs, each one weighing about 1.5 lb. (700 g), which is heavier than a grapefruit. The male incubates the eggs for about eight weeks, until the young chicks hatch. Their striped coloring provides effective camouflage.

How fast can an emu run? It can reach speeds of 30 mph (50 kmph).

An emu's booming call can be heard over 1.2 mi. (2 km) away.

Waterfowl

Waterfowl are birds that spend a large portion of their lives over, in, or using the water, either swimming or hunting. They have webbed feet to help them swim. They may also often have extra-waterproof feathers and, in many cases, specially adapted bills rather than beaks. They use a number of hunting techniques, such as diving, bobbing, or herding, to catch the fish that they eat.

Mallards are found throughout the northern hemisphere and have been introduced to Australia and New Zealand.

▼ What are the most common water birds?

Ducks and geese are perhaps the most familiar water birds. The mallard is the most widespread. In the winter, the male has his famous metallic green head, but in summer this turns brown, known as "eclipse" plumage. The females are brown and build down-lined nests on the ground or on slightly raised sites in which to lay their eggs. Their brown coloring provides camouflage for the female.

▼ How deep can a white-breasted cormorant dive?

A cormorant's feathers do not trap air in the same way that those of other birds do, and this allows them to dive more quickly and chase their prey underwater. They also have a hooked beak, well adapted for grasping and digging into fish. Underwater, they can propel themselves with their large webbed feet.

The white-breasted cormorant lives around the coast of Africa where it dives for fish, eels, and crustaceans.

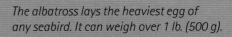
◄ Where do albatrosses nest?

Wandering albatrosses nest on small remote islands far out in the Southern Ocean. They prefer windswept areas, where the currents help them launch themselves into the air. Albatrosses use their huge wings to glide long distances on strong air currents, hardly beating their wings at all. In fact, they use far more energy in take off and landing. They feed mainly on squid and cuttlefish, sometimes diving under the water to catch their food.

How large is an Australian pelican's bill?

The Australian pelican's bill is the largest in the world and can reach up to a whopping 18 in. (47cm). What's most distinctive about the pelican bill, apart from its size, is the large pouch beneath it. Pelicans hunt in a group, herding fish into shallow water to be scooped into their bills. Pelicans are graceful flyers, too, often holding tight "V" formations, or swirling around in packs.

How much water can a pelican's bill hold? 24 pt. (11.5 l). That's more than their stomachs can hold.

Male and female pelicans cooperate in building their nests. The male brings the material and the female heaps it up to form a simple structure.

Shore Birds

Most shore birds have elongated toes to stop them from sinking into the mud or sand. They are usually long-legged and long-billed. Some beaks are straight, others are curved. They all tend to feed around water, some preferring rocky shores, some preferring sandy beaches, and others choosing muddy shallows or boggy marshes. Large groups of waders gather at high tides to feed at the water's edge.

Why do herons change color?

In the spring, many herons develop bright patterns on their legs and bills. Their facial skin may even "blush" slightly during courtship. These changes indicate that they are ready to breed. Like all herons, gray herons are primarily fish-eaters, but they will eat almost anything they can catch, including rats and frogs. They patiently watch their prey, attacking with a precise stab.

▶ Where do you find flamingos?

Flamingos are scattered all over the world, from southeastern Europe to South East Asia, Africa, and Central America. Like most flamingos, the greater flamingo nests in large colonies. They build up their nests from the mud on low-lying islands. These nests are vulnerable to flooding or, sometimes, to a drop in the water levels that allows predators to get closer over dry land. Some years they raise very few young, while other years there are "baby booms" that maintain their population.

▼ Why do curlews have long bills?

The curlew's long, down-curved bill is specially adapted to probe into wet mud for worms, insects, crabs, and mollusks that may live there. Curlews prefer shorelines and inland waters such as marshes and heath bogs, and can also be seen poking about in rock pools. They form flocks in the winter months and, in Europe in the spring, their song is one of the most attractive, which accelerates into a bubbling trill after a "cur-lew" sound, from which they are named.

 Curlews nest in shallow hollows that they line with grass and lay dark, speckled eggs that are camouflaged to look like a stone.

Flamingos are the only "filter-feeding" birds, which means they filter the water for food.

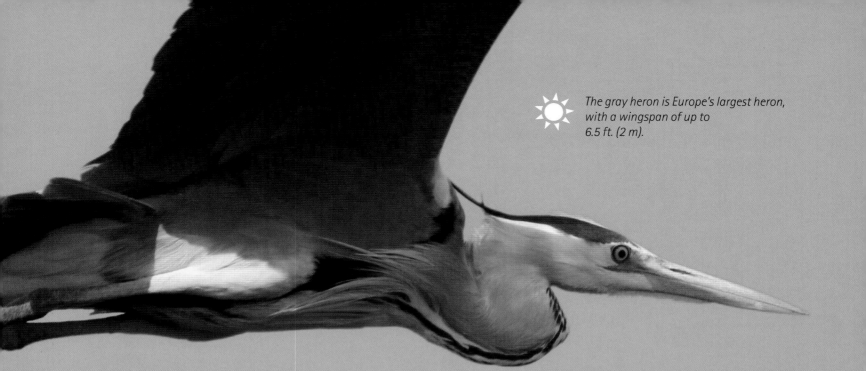

The gray heron is Europe's largest heron, with a wingspan of up to 6.5 ft. (2 m).

How many avocets do you get in a flock?
They can be tens of thousands strong.

Male avocets have a larger, squared, black wing tip than the females.

► What's special about an avocet's bill?

Avocets' bills turn upwards towards the end. If they find the right conditions, such as shallow salt water and oozing mud with drier islands scattered about, they will form larger, sprawling colonies, rather than packing tightly together like some other birds. But avocets are sociable and don't mind each other's company. They even jostle each other when feeding without too much irritation. When it feeds, the avocet leans forward on its long, blue-gray legs and sweeps its bill sideways through the water in order to find and catch small shrimp and marine worms.

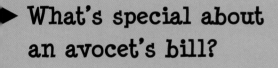

Birds of Prey

Many birds of prey, such as eagles and hawks, are strong hunters with large forward-facing eyes. This means they can sometimes see animals such as rabbits from as far away as 2 mi. (3.2 km) and are good at judging distances. They have hooked, powerful bills to tear open flesh and strong feet with sharp talons to catch prey. They are also often fast and skilled fliers and spend a lot of their time in the air.

▼ How do red kites fly?

Red kites are very light, agile fliers with a large, typically forked tail for manoeuvrability. In flight, the red kite flexes its wings and twists its long tail from side to side to use air currents to their fullest, although it doesn't usually go too high. It is also capable of fast stoops and twisting dives. Like the golden eagle, it also scavenges dead meat from sheep or rabbits, and will eat earthworms or insects.

Red kites take their name from the red-rust coloring on their forked tails and forewings.

Peregrines nest on broad ledges or scrapes on cliffs and quarries.

◀ How does a peregrine falcon hunt?

Peregrines mainly hunt other birds ranging in sizes from a starling or pigeon to a grouse. They are extremely fast and probably reach speeds higher than any other bird when dive-bombing their prey from above. As they dive, they fold in their wings and then reach out their claws on impact, sometimes catching them in mid-flight, other times striking them to the ground. They also approach birds from below or chase them in a level flight with acrobatic mid-air displays.

How big is a golden eagle?

olden eagles are powerful birds of prey
at have large wingspans of over 7.3 ft.
.2 m) and can weigh as
uch as 15 lb. (6.7 kg) as
adult. Despite their size,
ey can soar with great grace. Golden eagles
e their powerful vision to scan the sky for
rds, and the ground below for rabbits, dead
eep, grouse, and hares. Immature golden
gles can be identified by their black, slightly
ruffy-looking feathers. Adults have a paler,
wny head and dark brown plumage.

Golden eagles can live for 25 years. The female lays 1-3 eggs in February to June.

The kestrel can be found almost everywhere across the whole of Europe.

How fast is a peregrine falcon?
Diving, it can reach 117 mph (188 kmph).

Which bird of prey is most common in towns?

Kestrels are one of the most commonly seen
birds of prey in Europe and they are often
spotted on telephone poles or wires. Kestrels
hover in mid-air, as they scan the ground for
the voles, beetles, earthworms, and small
birds that make up their diet. They fan
their tails and beat their wings rapidly
to keep in one spot. They also use
their tails as a windbreak
when they land.

Parrots

Most parrots have large heads, short necks and legs, and many have brightly colored feathers. Their most identifiable feature is their bill, which has a broad base and a chisel-shaped cutting edge for cracking open seeds. Parrots also use their feet to hold and manipulate their food while eating.

▼ Which cockatoo gathers in huge flocks?

In Australia, large flocks of up to 2,000 sulfur crested cockatoos can gather to forage on grass, seeds, sprouting wheat, maize, and other grain. These flocks use a "sentinel" warning system, which means that, as the flock feeds, several individuals act as lookouts and raise the alarm if danger approaches by making screeches and raising the yellow crests on their heads. These cockatoos can damage crops and are considered pests by farmers. They also feed on nuts, berries, blossoms, and insect larvae, holding food with the foot and attacking or opening it with the powerful bill.

Cockatoos form mating pairs and share the incubation of eggs in tree hollows for 30 days.

▼ What are parakeets?

Parakeets are small or medium-sized parrots. The ring-necked parakeet, like many, is very adaptable. It lives in tropical Africa and Asia, where it can be found in a variety of woodland types, mangroves, open farmland, savannah grassland, and sometimes even parks and gardens. Like most parrots, parakeets often gather together in large groups and can cause damage to crops. Males have a blue, gray, and black coloring on their necks and cheeks, plus the rose-pink collar from which they take their name.

Ring-necked parakeets can be very noisy and annoying to those that live nearby.

▶ Where do budgerigars live in the wild?

In the wild, budgerigars live in semi-arid areas of Australia. They have a nomadic lifestyle, which means they move from place to place throughout the year and follow a general seasonal pattern of moving north in winter and south in summer. They breed at any time of the year, usually when there is a good supply of food. The birds nest in small hollows in tree trunks and sometimes share these with other couples.

Wild budgerigars are normally green or yellow, rather than blue.

How long have parrots been around?

Fossils of parrot-like birds date back to 40 million years ago.

Which bird of prey is most common in towns?

Scarlet macaws, like many types of parrot, gather near riverbanks in Central and South America to eat clay. It is thought that the birds gain vital minerals from the clay or it may neutralize the toxic affects of poisons from plants they have eaten, or both. Some Australian parrots have even been found with charcoal in their stomachs.

Macaws are the largest parrots and the scarlet macaw is the most numerous, but is under threat.

67

Nocturnal Birds

There are many types of nocturnal birds, including owls, nightjars, and frogmouths. All these birds hunt at night, and have soft wing feathers that allow them to fly silently. Owls have a rounded facial disk, made of short, stiff feathers, and big eyes on the front of their heads. This gives them excellent vision and depth perception. Nightjars' and frogmouths' eyes are on each side of their heads.

▼ Do owls only come out at night?

Owls usually hunt at night, but may change their behavior under certain pressures. Barn owls can sometimes be seen during the day in winter, and often hunt before dark in summer, especially if they have young to feed. Barn owls nest in holes in trees or in buildings and lay 4-7 eggs between May and June. They are found throughout Europe although they are not common, and eat voles, mice, rats, and occasionally small birds.

Like the barn owl, the tawny owl lives with its mate.

Which owl hoots after dark?

The tawny owl makes the familiar hooting sound, but it can also make other sounds and these are more often heard through the year. Tawny owls live in woods and nest in holes in trees or in buildings, but may take an old stick nest left by a crow or magpie. They carry their food in their beaks, unlike other birds of prey, which carry it in their talons.

Barn owls can have a wingspan of approximately 3 ft. (1 m).

►Where do nightjars make their nest?

Nightjars nest on the ground, where they scrape a clear patch in which to sit. They hunt insects and catch them in mid-flight using a broad, wide-open gaping beak. Nightjars hunt at dusk or dawn, when their distinctive, long "churr" call can be heard. They have camouflaged coloring similar to dead leaves or bark, which can make them very difficult to spot.

How long do tawny owls live? Up to 10 years.

 The nightjar is a solitary bird and does not gather in flocks.

 Tawny frogmouths mate for life and usually use the same nest each year, making repairs when needed.

◄ What is a frogmouth?

Frogmouths, like the tawny frogmouth, are related to nightjars. They live in forests or open woodlands and spend their days resting in tree trunks, where they are well camouflaged. At night, frogmouths ambush any prey that comes close to them from perches close to or even on the ground. They eat mainly insects, but sometimes catch frogs and mice.

Perching Birds

Perching birds form a large order of birds known as "passeriformes", which contains more than half of all known bird species. Most of these birds have slim, long toes that can grip well and lock together for security when perching on branches high up in trees. Most invest time and energy in raising their young, which are often blind and helpless when they hatch.

▼ What is a martin?

Martins spend much of their time flying through the air catching flying insects. Their feet are very small but are still strong enough to perch with, unlike swallows. House martins are most famous for building nests of saliva and mud in people's roof spaces. In some parts of Europe, they still nest in more remote places such as high mountain ledges. European birds often spend the winter in Africa.

A house martin's small, open nest is usually home to four or five chicks at a time.

What type of bird is a robin?

European robins are part of a group of perching birds called thrushes. They are generally quite stout, solid-built birds with large heads, big eyes, and short, strong bills. Robins live mainly in forests and woodland areas all over Europe and they have become highly adapted to follow larger animals as they rummage around the forest floor, churning up the mud. Robins then pick out the worms and insects that have been exposed.

Robins build domed nests of grasses and leaves, often in hedges, bushes, or thick ivy. They line them with moss and animal hair.

What is an ovenbird?

Ovenbirds are a type of bird found in Central America, so named because of the way they build their nests. They collect mud, straw, or dung, which they mix with saliva to make a nest in trees or on man-made objects such as posts or telephone poles. These nests look like a type of oven found in South America. The nests are impressive buildings with two chambers, one enclosed for containing and protecting the chicks, with a spiraling passageway that leads outside to an entrance that usually faces away from the wind.

The ovenbird is the national bird of Argentina.

How many ticks does an oxpecker eat in one day?
Oxpeckers can pick off around 100 ticks each day.

Why do oxpeckers peck at oxen?

Oxpeckers are useful birds for larger mammals as they pick lice and other parasites out of their fur or skin. They also remove skin and body fluids as well as cleaning around the edges of wounds. Oxpeckers have short legs and sharp claws that enable them to cling onto the fur or hide of the mammal, even if it is moving about. Oxpeckers are sociable birds that feed in flocks and return to communal roosts at night.

Oxpeckers build nests lined with animal hair in holes in trees, and lay 2-3 eggs.

Song Birds

To some extent, all birds are song birds. All birds make some form of noise or sound for a variety of reasons. These can range from more simple "calls" like that of the cuckoo or pigeon, which are closely related to perching birds, to the more complex "songs" of warblers. Their songs, like all birdsong, are created using a "syrinx", a sound box located in their necks, which is a little bit like our voicebox. However, it can pass air through two separate channels at once, producing different noises simultaneously. Birds change the pitch and volume by tightening and relaxing muscles in their necks.

Nightingales are commonly believed to have one of the finest singing voices and their song has inspired poets.

▼ Where do canaries live?

Canaries are a type of finch famous for their singing voices. Originally from the Azores, Madeira, and the Canary Islands, canaries are now popular pets all over the world. In the wild, canaries nest in orchards, or in trees and bushes. They have brown and gray streaks to their coloring, rather than the all-yellow of their captive cousins. They were first bred as pets by monks in the 1600s. Originally only males were sold, as they were more in demand for their singing voices.

The canary can take 30 mini breaths a second to replenish its air supply when singing.

◀ Do nightingales sing at night?

Nightingales are usually heard at dawn or dusk between the months of April and August, occasionally breaking into bursts of song during the day. They don't really sing during the night, but they can sometimes be heard just before night falls. Nightingales usually hide in thick undergrowth and vegetation close to the ground, where they search for worms, insect larvae, beetles, and berries.

▶ How many species of warbler are there?

There are around 400 species of warbler and most tend to migrate to breed. Their arrival in Europe coincides with the annual insect population increase in early summer, so there is plenty of food with which to feed their young. Warblers have probing beaks for picking caterpillars and aphids from bark and leaves, and for foraging for berries, spiders, and insects. Female marsh warblers lay six small, slightly camouflaged eggs in nests that hang from tall stems in dense vegetation.

The marsh warbler is the bird with the most songs, with 84 different variations or mimicked sounds.

When do most birds sing?
At dawn, although exactly why is not fully understood.

What does the red-eyed vireo's song sound like?

The red-eyed vireo can sometimes sound like it is endlessly repeating the same question and answer over and over again. Vireos are similar to warblers but have heavier bills. They breed mainly in North America, where they can fall victim to a bird called the brown-headed cowbird. This is a nest parasite that lays its eggs in other birds' nests so the victims raise the chick as their own.

The red-eyed vireo can sing its song thousands of times over the course of a day.

Bandicoots, Wombats, and Quolls

Marsupials are a group of mammals with a pouch on their bellies, which they use to carry around their young. Inside the pouch, the marsupial's baby is safe, and can drink its mother's milk from a teat. Marsupials are a very old order of animals, and one hundred million years ago they lived all over the world. Today, almost all species of marsupial are found in Australia, where there is no threat from larger, more successful mammals.

▼ What is a quoll?

A quoll is a cat-sized marsupial found in Australia, Tasmania, and New Guinea. There are several different species, all with spotted coats. They are all meat-eaters, mainly hunting mice, lizards, and snakes. When a quoll is born, it is no bigger than a grain of rice. There are usually 10 babies in a litter, but only the strongest six survive, as the mother only has six teats in her pouch. Baby quolls stay in the pouch for several months.

▼ What do bandicoots look like?

Bandicoots are medium-sized marsupials that live in Australia and New Guinea. They have long back legs, and move by hopping about. A bandicoot's big ears and excellent hearing help it find prey at night, and listen out for predators in the dark. The long-nosed bandicoot uses its long snout to search for food. It digs holes in the earth with its front paws, and then sniffs out insects and pulls up roots.

Long-nosed bandicoots are born after a pregnancy of just 12 days. They grow inside their mother's pouch, drinking her milk for about two months.

Quolls are now endangered, because modern farming techniques are destroying their natural habitat.

A wombat's teeth are like a rodent's in that they never stop growing, and are worn down by constant plant-chewing.

Which kind of marsupial lives in the Americas?

possums are the only kind of marsupial
live in North and South America,
all other marsupials are found in
ustralia and New Guinea. Some species
opossum have pouches, but others don't.
ost opossums live in forests, climbing
es to hunt insects. An opossum will wrap
long, hairless tail around a branch to stop
from falling. The Virginia opossum has a very
teresting defense tactic. When faced with a serious
reat, it lies still, pretending to be dead. This puts
e predator off, and the Virginia opossum makes
quick escape.

*Most species of opossum
are about 3 ft. (1 m) long,
with a very long rat-like tail.*

How many species of marsupial are there? There are about 272 species of marsupial in the world, and about 200 of them are found in Australia.

Where do wombats live?

Wombats are ground-dwelling marsupials that live in Australia. They are large, tailless animals, measuring up to 4 ft. (1.2 m) long, which is about as big as a pig. Wombats are the world's biggest burrowing animals. The common wombat digs a complex system of tunnels with its strong legs and long claws. It usually lives alone in its big burrow. At night, the common wombat emerges to feed on grasses, roots, and fungi.

Kangaroos and Koalas

Some of the world's most interesting wildlife is found in Australia, where well over half of all species of marsupial live. Magnificent red kangaroos are some of the fastest animals on land. Their smaller relatives, the wallabies, also roam vast areas of Australian grassland. Other memorable and unique Australian marsupials include the sleepy, leaf-munching koala and the fierce, noisy Tasmanian devil.

▼ How far can kangaroos jump?

The red kangaroo is an incredible jumper. A male red kangaroo can cover over 25 ft. (8 m) in a single leap, which is almost the width of a swimming pool. Their long tails help them balance as they bound along on their powerful hind legs. Young kangaroos, called joeys, are only about 0.75 in. (2 cm) long when they are born. That's about twice the length of your fingernail. When they are born, they crawl into their mother's pouch, and latch onto a teat.

Kangaroos live in the Australian grasslands. They spend their days resting and feed on plants at dusk and during the night, when the temperature is cooler.

Do all kangaroos live on the ground? No, some, like the small tree kangaroos, live high up in the branches of rainforest trees.

The red-necked wallaby was one of the first marsupials to be seen by the European settlers who landed in Sydney Cove, Australia, in 1788.

◄ Are wallabies and kangaroos related?

Wallabies are members of the kangaroo family. Like kangaroos, wallabies have strong back legs and can leap fast across open grassland. When they want to move slowly, they drop down onto all fours. Both wallabies and kangaroos begin life as tiny, bean-sized babies inside their mother's pouch. Red-necked wallabies are sometimes called brushers, because they are found in wooded areas and brush rather than rolling, open grassland. They are quite common in the coastal forests of eastern and southeastern Australia.

Is a koala a bear?

o, the koala is actually a marsupial, not a bear.
ke other marsupials, koalas carry their small babies
pouches. When a koala baby outgrows its pouch,
hitches a ride on its mother's back as she clambers
rough the trees. Koalas are very fussy eaters and
ill only eat the leaves and bark of eucalyptus trees.
hey spend their lives eating and sleeping in the
eetops, only coming down to the ground to move
ong to another clump of trees.

Koalas sleep for approximately 18 hours per day.

How noisy are devils?

Tasmanian devils are famous for the blood-curdling shrieks and growls they make as they gather in groups around a carcass, such as a dead wombat or wallaby. They usually eat at night, searching for food with their keen senses of sight and smell.

Tasmanian devils were once found across Australia but now only live on the island of Tasmania. They are the top predators there.

Sloths, Anteaters, and Armadillo

Sloths are in the same animal order as anteaters and armadillos. They are grouped together because they all have few or no teeth. Sloths eat leaves and fruit in the South American rainforests. The anteaters of Central and South America survive on a diet of insects, such as ants and termites. Armadillos are omnivorous. Unlike sloths and anteaters, their bodies are covered with tough, bony plates, which protect them from predators.

▼ Which species of armadillo is the most common?

The nine-banded armadillo from North, Central, and South America is the most common. In spite of its name, it may have 7-11 bands of armor around its body, with an extra 12-15 rings around its tail. To escape trouble, the nine-banded armadillo can run faster than a dog. Nine-banded armadillos dig burrows, in which they rest during the day. They often share their burrow with other armadillos of the same sex, and even with other animals, such as rabbits and skunks.

▼ How long is a giant anteater's tongue?

A giant anteater's tongue is an impressive 2 ft. (60 cm) long, which is about ten times longer than your tongue. It is covered with small spines, which point backwards. The anteater's saliva makes these spines sticky, so they are very good at mopping up insects. Giant anteaters do not live in trees, like their smaller relatives. They live in the forests and grasslands of Central and South America, and are active during the day.

Giant anteaters walk on their knuckles, so their long claws stay sharp for digging.

Some armadillos roll into a ball when threatened, while others defend themselves with their sharp front claws, or simply bolt for cover in their burrows.

Where do giant armadillos live?

Giant armadillos live in the Amazon
Basin in South America. They can
survive in many different habitats,
including rainforest and grassland.
They are solitary creatures, only coming
together to breed. Giant armadillos are
the biggest armadillos. They are almost
3 ft. (1 m) long, and weigh about 57
lb. (26 kg), which is about as heavy as
a large dog. This large animal's diet
is mainly made up of tiny ants and
termites, so it needs to eat a lot of
them to satisfy its appetite.

The giant armadillo can stand
upright on its hind legs and tail
to reach up into tall termite
mounds. It will also stand like
this to warn off predators.

How big are sloths?

Sloths are quite small animals. The southern
two-toed sloth is about the size and shape of
a small dog. It has a small, round head, a short
neck, and long limbs. Baby two-toed sloths are
just 10 in. (25 cm) long, which is about the same
size as a rabbit. Unlike most furry animals, sloths
don't groom or clean their fur. Tiny green
plants, called algae, grow on a sloth's fur.
This provides excellent camouflage as
the sloth hangs still in the branches
of a tree.

How do sloths hang onto branches? Sloths hook their strong
claws over branches so they can hang upside down from them.

Bats and Flying Mammals

Bats are the only mammals that can fly through the air like birds. Some mammals, such as the sugar glider of Australia and the flying lemur of South East Asia, can glide between trees, but do not actually fly. Over one quarter of all the different species of mammals in the world are bats. Amazingly, there are over 950 bat species.

The pipistrelle bat is common in Europe and eats insects. Its tiny body would fit inside a matchbox.

▼ How do sugar gliders move?

Sugar gliders are small, squirrel-like mammals that live in the forests of Australia and New Guinea. They have a very quick way of moving to the next tree by simply jumping off a branch and opening out their flaps of skin to catch the air, like a parachute. They can then glide down to a lower branch, landing safely on all fours. Sugar gliders are marsupials. The female has a pouch, in which she carries her newborn baby. The baby is tiny at birth, and remains in the pouch for about 10 weeks.

▲ Which bat is the smallest?

The world's smallest bat is the hog-nosed bat, sometimes called the "bumblebee bat". This rare species lives in Thailand in South East Asia. Its wings measure just 6 in. (15 cm), and its body is about the size of a walnut. Most species of bat only have one baby at a time. A baby bat, called a cub, is carried by its mother for the first few weeks of life, but it is soon too heavy for this. It learns to fly at about four weeks old, and begins to hunt on its own.

Sugar gliders nest in groups of up to seven related couples and their babies.

Do bats fly by day? Almost all bats are nocturnal. During the day, they sleep upside down, or roost in caves or hollow trees.

What are flying lemurs?

Flying lemurs are mammals that can glide between trees. They are not related to the lemurs of Madagascar, nor can they really fly. Like bats, they are nocturnal, and roost upside down in the rainforest trees of South East Asia. They eat fruit, leaves, and flowers. Flying lemurs carry their young until they become independent. A female flying lemur takes her baby with her as she glides between the trees.

 Flying lemurs are also called colugos. The flaps of skin that stretch down each side of their bodies from neck to tail look like a cloak.

◄ How do fruit bats find their food?

Bats have better hearing than most other mammals, but poor eyesight. Many species have unusually large ears, to capture the slightest vibration in the air. Most kinds of bat hunt insects. They make tiny squeaking noises, which bounce back when they touch a flying insect. The bat can then work out exactly where the insect is and snap it up. Some fruit-eating bats are known as "flying foxes". They have big eyes, long snouts and furry faces, which may have earned them this name. They find their food by smell.

 A bat's wings are made of thin skin, stretched tightly between its legs, tail, arms, and fingers.

Rabbits and Hares

Rabbits and hares are small, furry mammals with long ears, short tails, and powerful back legs for speedy running. Like rodents, they have big front teeth, which never stop growing, and they eat grass, roots, and leaves. Rabbits, hares, and another little mammal called the pika are all members of the lagomorph order. There are about 79 species in this order of animals.

▼ Where do hares live?

Hares do not dig or live in underground burrows, like rabbits. Instead, they live in open countryside. Hares make a shallow trench in long grass, called a form, where they take shelter and rest. They are well camouflaged in their form, so long as they keep absolutely still. Baby hares, called leverets, are born above ground, so need to be active and alert from the start. They are born covered in fur, with their eyes open, and can stand and walk just minutes after they are born.

 A female hare is called a jill, and a male is called a jack.

Is the black-tailed jackrabbit a true rabbit?

The black-tailed jackrabbit is actually a hare. It lives in many parts of North America, and is considered a pest by farmers, because it will often eat and damage their crops. During the breeding season, male hares put on fascinating displays to attract the attention of females. They chase each other, leap up in the air, and box each other in fights.

What's a pika's closest relative?

The pika is a small, plant-eating mammal that lives in Asia and North America. It is related to the rabbit, but is much smaller. The large-eared pika is found in the mountainous forests of the Himalayas in Asia. It is about 8 in. (20 cm) long, about the same size as a guinea pig. The pika is a very well-organized little creature. In summer, when it has plenty of food, it sets aside stems of grass, letting them dry in the sun. It then piles the dry grass into miniature haystacks. When winter comes and food is scarce, the pika makes good use of its special food store.

Pikas are also known as mouse hares or conies. North American species often shelter in the gaps between rocks.

How fast can hares run? The North American jackrabbit can reach speeds of 50 mph (80 kmph), which is almost the speed limit on U.S.A roads.

The black-tailed jackrabbit's long ears help it control its temperature and cool down in the fierce heat of the North American deserts.

▼ Do rabbits live in groups?

Rabbits are sociable animals, living in family groups of about 10 adults and their young kittens. They dig a system of burrows called a warren. There are many separate entrances into the warren, and quick escape routes. A rabbit prefers to nibble grass and other plants at dusk, or during the night, spending the rest of its time underground in the warren. Rabbits are hunted by many different animals and are on constant guard against predators.

A female rabbit, called a doe, can give birth seven times a year, and may have up to 10 babies in each litter.

Small Rodents

Almost half of all the mammal species in the world are rodents. Members of this successful animal family are found in every continent except Antarctica, and live in a variety of habitats, from hot deserts to frozen tundra. All rodents have long, sharp front teeth, which are used for gnawing. Some rodents are small, for example, mice, rats, cavies, and lemmings.

▼ Where do mice live?

There are many different species of mouse, living in a range of habitats, for example, in temperate woodland, tropical rainforest, and open grassland. The house mouse is the only species that makes close contact with people. All other species keep well away from human settlements. Newborn mice are very small and completely defenseless, being born bald, deaf, and blind. But in just two weeks, they are bold enough to go exploring. They are ready to have babies of their own at just six weeks old.

 Many species of mouse are excellent climbers, such as the harvest mouse. This tiny mouse makes its nest above ground level on grass stems and wheat stalks. It holds on tight with its long, gripping tail.

▼ How many brown rats are there?

There are more than 50 species of rat, but the two most common ones are the brown and the black rat. Black rats live in warm climates, but brown rats are more adaptable and are found in almost every country. No one knows exactly how many rats there are, but there may be billions, maybe even one rat for every one person on Earth. Wild rats carry about 30 infectious diseases, which can be picked up by humans. Rats can also damage crops, perhaps wrecking up to a fifth of all the world's crops every year. It is hardly surprising that wild rats are considered vermin.

 Black and brown rats have up to 22 babies in a litter, and may have seven litters in a single year. This means that every female rat can produce up to 154 babies a year.

What are lemmings?

Lemmings are a kind of vole, which is a group of over 150 rodent species. Voles have blunter faces, stockier bodies, and shorter legs and tails than their mouse relatives. Lemmings live in the far north of America, Europe, and Asia. They have very thick fur, and survive the winter cold by burrowing under the snow to find plants to eat. Large numbers of lemmings live together in burrows or crevices in rock. When their food supply runs out, usually every three or four years, they migrate in big crowds to find new sources of food.

Why do rodents have so many babies? Lots of animals eat rodents, so they have large litters to increase their chances of survival.

Many popular household pets are rodents, for example, gerbils, hamsters, and guinea pigs. Gerbils come from Africa and Asia; hamsters from Europe and Asia; and guinea pigs from South America.

What are cavies?

Wild guinea pigs are called cavies. They are small, tailless rodents that live in the grassland and deserts of South America. Cavies can see, walk, and run from the day they are born. This is important, because they are hunted by many predators, such as weasels and birds of prey. Humans also hunt them for their meat. Domestic guinea pigs are now kept as pets all over the world.

Elephants and Hyraxes

Elephants are the biggest and heaviest land animals alive today. There are two species of elephant, the African and Asian elephant. Surprisingly, perhaps, the elephant's closest living relative is an animal called the hyrax. This little furry mammal is no bigger than a pet cat, just a fraction of the elephant's size.

It is easy to tell African and Asian elephants apart by the shape of their ears. African elephants have large, rounded ears, while Asian elephants have smaller, triangular ears.

What do hyraxes and elephants have in common?

The hyrax is a small mammal that looks like a rodent, but is actually related to the elephant. Both elephants and hyraxes have tusks, and nails on their padded feet. Millions of years ago, elephants and hyraxes were both enormous. The hyrax got smaller as it adapted to its changing environment, but the elephant didn't.

▲ Where do African elephants live?

African elephants live in all sorts of different environments, from the forests of central Africa to the deserts of Namibia. Different species of African elephant are found in different habitats. The bush elephant lives in grassland, the smaller forest elephant lives in woodland, and the rare desert elephant lives in dry, hot deserts. The forest elephant is the smallest of all African elephants. This smaller size makes it easier to move between the trees. All kinds of elephant lose heat through their ears, and the bush elephant of the hot savannah needs big ears to lose as much heat as possible. The ears of a forest elephant are smaller, because it lives in a cooler habitat.

There are seven species of hyrax. Some live in rocky mountain areas; others prefer forests. Hyraxes live in family groups, like elephants.

◀ Do elephants live alone?

Female elephants live in herds, led by an old female called a matriarch. The matriarch's herd includes her own young, and her older daughters and their families. Female elephant herds often stay together for many years. When a male elephant is about ten years old, it leaves its first herd. Young male elephants form their own herds, but they are not loyal to one particular herd. A male elephant may change herds many times in its long life.

Young elephants are looked after by all the females in the herd. This helps the mother and allows the other young females to learn mothering skills.

Where do Asian elephants live?

Very few Asian elephants are left in the wild. They live in remote, mountainous forests in South East Asia. Like all species of elephant, Asian elephants can travel long distances to find food and water. These journeys, called migrations, happen twice a year and always follow the same route. An elephant's long trunk is boneless and very flexible. It is used for breathing, smelling, and drinking. It is both strong and extremely sensitive. It can pull a tough branch off a tree or pick up a tiny object from the ground.

Asian elephants can be tamed, and have been used for centuries to tow logs and clear forests. In South East Asia, they are decorated for festival processions.

How do elephants keep cool? They flap their ears, roll in mud, and splash in water.

Horses

Wild horses were first tamed in Asia over 6,000 years ago. Today, there are no truly wild species of horse left in their natural habitat. The Przewalski's horse no longer survives in the wild, and is only found in zoos and wildlife reserves. There are, however, many herds of feral horses roaming free around the world. Feral horses are descendants of tame horses, that escaped from their owners.

▼ What kind of mammal is an ass?

An ass is a wild relative of the horse. There are three kinds of ass, the African, the kulan, and kiang. Asses live in dry, rocky places, and can survive on very little water. They eat tough, spiky grass to survive in this barren environment. Asian wild asses are hunted by wolves. They live in large herds. When they are threatened, a group of strong males gets together to chase away the predators.

▼ Where did the Przewalski's horse live in the wild?

The Przewalski's horse lived in herds on the high grasslands of Mongolia. Today, it is extinct in this habitat, and there are only about 1,600 left in captivity. Attempts are being made to reintroduce this species into the wild. The Przewalski's horse is smaller and stockier than most domestic and feral horses. But, like all horses, it has very sharp senses. It can see, smell, and hear extremely well, and can detect a threat from a great distance.

The Asian wild ass grazes on grass, but will also eat herbs and even the bark of trees when food is scarce.

All members of the horse family have one baby at a time, called a foal. Foals can walk just a few minutes after birth.

How many breeds of horses and ponies are there? There are over 350 different breeds in total.

Male adult horses are called stallions, and female adults are called mares. Young females are fillies, and young males are colts.

The zebra's black and white coat breaks up its outline, confusing predators by making it hard to spot.

▲ Where do feral horses live?

Feral horses are descended from domestic horses, but they run free in many different habitats, such as dry plains, savannah, wetlands, mountains, and even in deserts. All feral horses eat grass, which grows around the world. Australia has more feral horses than any other continent. The horses are called "brumbies" and roam throughout Australia's many different habitats. Many herds of feral horses, called mustangs, are also found in the U.S.A.

Is the zebra a kind of horse?

Zebras are members of the horse family They are smaller than horses, but are a similar shape and have the same kind of feet, which have soft toes hidden behind hard hooves. Like horses, zebras eat grass. Zebras are found in Africa, on grassland south of the Sahara. They live in small family groups and, when there is plenty of food and water, several groups will join together to form a herd.

Rhinos and Tapirs

Rhinoceroses and tapirs are closely related to each other, although they look very different. Both have three toes on each foot, and are quiet, solitary plant-eaters. Both kinds of mammal are quite rare, because they have been over-hunted by humans and their habitat is threatened. Rhinos live in Africa and parts of South East Asia, and tapirs live in Central and South America, and also in South East Asia.

Rhino horns are made of hair, not bone. These hairs are tightly packed together to make the horn hard and tough.

▲ Are white rhinos white?

White rhinos are gray-brown in color. The "white" in their name comes from a word in Afrikaans, a South African language. This word means "wide" and describes the animal's broad lips. White rhinos graze on grass with their wide lips. Female white rhinos give birth to one calf every two years and look after it until the next one is born. She can produce up to 44 pt. (20 l) of milk a day to feed her baby. Rhino calves may be hunted by lions or hyenas.

◄ Where do black rhinos come from?

Black rhinos are found in central and southern Africa. Their hooked lips and sharp horns make them look fierce, but they eat plants and do not hunt other animals. Black rhinos pull leaves from trees and bushes with their flexible upper lips. Black rhinos usually live alone, and do not like intruders on their territory. They are fairly short-sighted, and will charge at any moving thing that they don't like or recognize. To make up for their poor sight, black rhinos have good senses of hearing and smell.

Rhinos are different from all other horned animals, because their horns are near their mouths, not on top of their heads. They are famous for their thick skin, which hangs over their bodies like a leathery suit of armor.

Why do tapirs have long snouts?

A tapir's snout is made up of its nose and upper lip. It is very useful for grasping vegetation to bite off and chew. Tapirs eat shoots and leafy plants that grow on the forest floor. All tapir babies have coats that are covered in a pattern of spots and stripes. This breaks up their outline and makes them hard to see in the rainforest shadows. As the babies grow, this distinctive pattern fades and disappears.

How big is the white rhino? The white rhino is the second-largest land animal on Earth after the elephant. It weighs over two tons.

Which tapir is the biggest?

The Malaysian tapir is the biggest species of tapir. It can grow up to 8.4 ft. (2.5 m) long, about the size of a donkey. All tapirs have heavy, short-legged bodies, so they can push through undergrowth in the dense rainforests where they live. Tapirs are good swimmers and they never stray far from water. They are hunted by big cats and, if threatened, they plunge into the water and swim.

Tapirs can stay underwater for some time, because they use their long snouts as a kind of snorkel to breathe the air.

Pigs, Peccaries, and Hippos

Wild pigs and peccaries are small, strong mammals with short legs and heavy bodies. The hippopotamus is related to the pig and, despite its large size, it does not eat meat, preferring instead to munch grasses. Pigs, peccaries, and hippos are very good at defending themselves. Wild pigs in South East Asia can stab tigers with their tusks, peccaries in South America will take on jaguars, and a hippo will fight a crocodile if needed.

 Collared peccaries take their name from the band of white fur around their necks. Their tusks are shorter than those of wild pigs, but still long enough to protect them.

▼ Do hippos like water?

The name hippopotamus means "river horse". Hippos spend most of the day in rivers, lakes, and ponds across Africa. They keep most of their bodies underwater, to keep cool and avoid getting sunburnt. They leave the water at night to graze on grasses, which they crop with their hard lips. Hippos are sociable creatures, living in groups of up to 15 animals. Baby hippos weigh about 120 lb. (55 kg) when they are born, and struggle to their feet only minutes after birth. They stay close to their mothers at all times, for protection against predators.

The pygmy hippo's body is narrower and more slender than the common hippo.

How long can hippos stay underwater?

The common hippo can stay underwater for as long as 10 minutes.

Where do peccaries live?

Peccaries are medium-sized mammals that look similar to pigs, and even behave like them, but they are not close relatives. They live in Central and South America. Peccaries live in large herds and will defend themselves as a group, turning together on a predator, such as a big cat. Sometimes a single peccary will charge at an enemy, sacrificing itself to allow the rest of the herd to escape.

Where do wild boars live?

Wild boars live in many countries around the world, usually in forests. They have a coarse coat of brown or gray fur, which hides them well among the trees. Although wild boars have a reputation for being dirty, they will only wallow in mud occasionally, to keep cool. Female wild boars, called sows, give birth to litters of five or six piglets in grass-lined burrows. Newborn piglets are completely helpless, and stay in their burrow for several days before venturing out. Their coats are stripy, to provide camouflage and give protection from predators.

Wild boars have sharp tusks, which are actually canine teeth that curve upwards out of their mouths.

Why do warthogs have such big tusks?

Warthogs have very long tusks, which are sometimes used to fight off predators. They are also used to dig up food, such as plant roots, in the hard earth. During the mating season, male warthogs use their tusks to fight each other. Common warthogs live on the plains of Africa, in family groups called sounders. They have three pairs of warts on their faces and a dark mane that runs down their backs. Their eyesight is poor, but they have a good sense of hearing and smell.

Warthogs sometimes eat their own dung and the dung of other animals, such as hippos.

Cattle

Cattle are large, plant-eating animals that live in countries all over the world. The first cattle were tamed, or domesticated, about 5,000 years ago. Today, wild species of cattle, such as the bison, musk oxen, and gaur, are becoming increasingly rare. There are about 200 different breeds of domestic cattle and most are farmed for their milk, meat, and hides, although some are still used to pull heavy loads and plough fields.

All species of cattle have four stomachs, to help them digest their food. Grass takes about three or four days to pass through a bison's digestive system.

▲ Are bison endangered?

North American bison were once very common and lived in herds of up to 100,000 individuals. Unfortunately, they were hunted by European settlers to such an extent that only about 1,000 remained. Today, the numbers of bison have increased again, because herds are kept on specially managed farms. American bison are strange-looking creatures, with huge, stocky shoulders and large heads. Male bison fight for females during the breeding season. They lock heads and push together. The winner is the one that forces the other one backwards. For most of the year, male and female bison live apart in small groups. They spend their time grazing on grasses and plants.

▼ How do musk oxen keep warm?

Musk oxen live on the tundra, the frozen treeless plains of the Arctic. They have thick, shaggy coats of fur, which stop them from freezing to death in the sub-zero temperatures. Musk oxen use their long, downward-curving horns in self-defense. If a herd of musk oxen is attacked by a pack of Arctic wolves, the adults protect their young by standing around them in a circle. They then lower their heads to form a ring of threatening horns.

Musk oxen have extra large hooves to stop them from sinking into the snow.

A herd of gaurs is led by a single dominant bull. A gaur's position in a herd depends on how big it is. The smaller the gaur, the lower its ranking in the group.

Where do water buffalo live?

Water buffalo are found in the wetter parts of Asia and also in Europe, northern Africa, South America, and northern Australia. They were once very common in the wild, but now are mainly kept as working farm animals. The broad hooves and strong legs of water buffalo make them good at wading though mud and swamps. For many centuries, they have been used to farm flooded rice fields in southern Asia. Like other domestic cattle, water buffalo are also kept for milking.

 The water buffalo has the longest horns of any animal alive today, measuring around 4 ft. (1.2 m) long.

Which is the biggest animal in North America? The bison. It weighs more than a small car.

Where do gaurs live?

Gaurs are wild cattle that live in South East Asia, from Nepal and India across to Malaysia. They rest at night in forests, moving by day into grassy clearings to feed. These shy, peaceful creatures are hunted by tigers.

Gaurs live in herds of up to 40 animals and communicate with each other using a number of different sounds, including snorts and growls.

Goats and Sheep

Goats and sheep are in a family of animals called bovidae. Cattle and antelopes are also in this family. All bovids have horns on their heads, which keep growing throughout the animal's life. Goats and sheep have been domesticated for thousands of years. There are many different domestic breeds, but species of wild sheep and goats still live around the world, particularly in mountain areas.

Wild goats, such as the mountain ibex, have hooves that are specially designed for climbing. These hooves have hard edges and soft, rubbery centers, which have good grip on slippery rocks.

▲ Where do Alpine ibexes live?

Alpine ibexes live in mountain areas of southern Europe, northern Africa, and as far east as northern India. During the day, they climb mountain slopes to feed, but by night, they move down to the lower forests to rest. These goats will feed on grasses, leaves, shoots, and bark. In winter, when mountains are covered with a thick blanket of snow, there is no food for the alpine ibex to eat. It moves down to the valleys to graze on the lower pastures.

Female mountain goats give birth to their babies, called kids, on steep cliffs. This helps them to avoid predators. Newborn kids become mobile very quickly, to stay out of danger.

◀ Why are mountain goats white?

Mountain goats have a coat of white wool, which grows especially thick during the winter. The white color provides good camouflage on the snowy mountain slopes of North America, where the mountain goat lives. The main predator of the mountain goat is the mountain lion. Mountain goats tend to live alone in summer and form large herds in the winter. The sure-footed mountain goat makes its way slowly and carefully through the thick snow, rarely losing its footing on the icy rocks.

Which sheep have spiral horns?

ighorn sheep live in the Rocky Mountains of North merica. Like some other wild sheep, bighorn sheep ave long, broad horns, which grow in a spiral at the des of their head. A ram's horns give away his age, ealth, and how good he is at fighting. Male bighorn eep fight by charging at each other at speeds of up 20 mph (32 kmph). They will do this about five times n hour, sometimes for as long as 24 hours, until one f the fighters becomes exhausted and retreats.

Bighorn sheep use rocky footholds that are only 2 in. (5 cm) wide, and can jump up to 20 ft. (6 m) between ledges.

How many domestic sheep are there in the world today?

There are around 800 million domestic sheep, and over 800 different breeds.

The largest flocks of domestic sheep in the world are in Australia, where there are over 140 million sheep.

Which wild sheep is the smallest?

The mouflon is one of the world's smallest wild sheep. It lives in southwestern Asia and southern Europe. This little sheep was first tamed about 9,000 years ago, and is the ancestor of today's domestic sheep. Like other wild sheep, the mouflon grows a thick coat of wool every winter, to keep it warm and dry. In the summer, the mouflon sheds its wool to stay cool.

Deer and Antelopes

Deer and antelopes are grazing and browsing animals. They are adapted to running, so they're good at escaping from danger. Their keen senses help them detect predators at a distance, so they have time to get away. Many species have impressive antlers or long, curved horns on their heads. There are about 36 kinds of deer and over 100 kinds of antelope.

Male deer are called stags, females are called hinds, and babies are called fawns. They eat leaves and grass for up to 12 hours a day.

Which species of antelope is the biggest?

The eland of central and southern Africa is the biggest species of antelope, measuring up to 6.6 ft. (2 m) tall at the shoulder. This large mammal is well adapted to the hot climate, and doesn't need to drink often, because it gets plenty of water from the plants it eats.

▲ How big are red deer?

An adult male red deer has a shoulder height of about 4.4 ft. (1.3 m) and is one of the biggest mammals in Europe. For most of the year, male and female red deer live separately, but they meet together during the mating season. Male red deer fight each other to win a mate. This is called rutting. Older males have larger antlers and win most fights, securing a more dominant position in the herd.

Despite its large size, the eland is surprisingly agile. It can jump over high fences.

◄ Why do springboks jump?

Like many kinds of antelope, the springbok is very agile, and can jump high into the air to avoid predators. The acrobatic springbok can leap as high as 11.6 ft. (3.5 m), quite a feat for an animal that is only 31 in. (80 cm) tall. Springboks live in herds and are constantly watching for predators, such as lions, before stalking them through the long grass. Like other antelopes, male springboks have long, curved horns.

What are antlers made of? Antlers are made of bone and are covered with a velvety skin. Each year, they are shed and a new set grows.

Do moose live in herds?

The moose is the largest kind of deer, measuring up to 6 ft. 9 in. (2.1 m) at the shoulder. Unlike other deer, the moose is a solitary animal, living alone except during the breeding season. Moose are found in the forests of North America, and in Europe, where they are known as elks. A moose's huge, flattened antlers make it look fierce, but the animal is a peaceful plant-eater. In winter, it survives on a diet of roots, bark, and leaves, and in the summer it will wade into shallow rivers and lakes to graze on water plants.

The size of a deer's antlers shows how old it is. A bull's antlers indicate its rank within the population.

Pronghorns and Giraffes

Pronghorns do not have any close mammal relatives and are classified in a family of their own. They are only found in western North America. Giraffes are one of the most unusual animals on Earth. They are so tall that they can see for miles around. These giants of the African savannah tower over their smaller relatives, the okapis, which live in the rainforests of central Africa.

Okapis cannot see very well, but have excellent hearing and sense of smell.

▼ What's special about pronghorns?

The pronghorn is unique, as it is the only animal of its type. It looks like an antelope, but it is not a member of this animal family. Pronghorns have distinctive sharp horns that are shaped like meat prongs. Females also have horns, but they are much shorter than the horns of males. Pronghorns live in deserts and grassland, browsing on vegetation. In the autumn and winter, pronghorns form large herds of up to 1,000 animals.

▲ What's related to a giraffe?

The okapi looks a bit like a horse, but it is actually the giraffe's nearest relative. This shy mammal lives in the rainforest, and does not have the long, thin legs and neck of its savannah cousin. Okapis have the same-shaped heads, and the same short, stubby horns, thin lips and long, grasping tongue as their giraffe cousins. Okapis are solitary animals that stay in a small area of their natural habitat for all their lives. They keep to well-trodden paths through the forest, as they search for leaves, buds, and shoots to eat.

Pronghorns are the fastest mammal in North and South America, reaching speeds of up to 54 mph (86 kmph).

The giraffe has a long, grasping tongue, which it uses to pull down the highest leaves from the tallest branches.

◀ What's the tallest animal in the world?

The giraffe is the world's tallest animal, measuring a staggering 20 ft. (6 m) from head to foot. It has such long front legs that it has to spread them apart to drink at waterholes. When it feeds, a giraffe can reach the top of an acacia tree, tearing off the thorny twigs with its tough mouth. Adult giraffes have only two main enemies, which are lions and humans. However, young giraffes may fall prey to leopards, hyenas, or crocodiles. Giraffes aim sharp kicks at predators to defend themselves, or else simply run away from trouble.

Why do giraffes have long tails? Giraffes have long tails to flick away irritating insects.

Giraffes can run at speeds of almost 30 mph (50 kmph).

How long are giraffes pregnant for?

A female giraffe is pregnant for about 15 months before she gives birth to a single calf. Only an hour or so after its birth, the calf can follow its mother across the grassland. Giraffes live in small groups of females and their young, led by one male. Males will fight each other to become leader of a group.

Small Cats

Domestic cats are very popular pets, and there are over 500 million pet cats in the world today. Cats that live in the wild are much fiercer than their tame relatives. There are 37 kinds of wild cat, and most of these species are quite small, such as the serval, ocelot, lynx, and caracal. Many wild cats have been hunted for their beautiful coats, and now need to be protected in their natural environment.

▼ Why do servals have long legs?

The serval is a small cat with very long legs, so it can pounce on its prey in the grasslands where it lives. This species of cat hunts small rodents and ground-nesting birds, and is able to jump over the tall grass to catch them. Servals have sensitive hearing and locate their prey by sound. Servals live in the grasslands of central and western Africa. They usually live near water, where leafy bushes grow to hide them from predators. A serval's spotted fur provides camouflage as it sits in the shade.

 The serval can leap up to 10 ft. (3 m) into the air to catch ground-nesting birds, such as francolins.

Lynx have large, round paws, which help them walk over the snow without sinking in.

▲ Which cat lives in three continents?

The lynx lives in the mountain ranges of North America, Asia, and Europe. A female lynx always gives birth in spring, so her cubs are strong enough to survive the next winter. Lynxes have unusually short tails and tufted ears, which make them look different from other cats. In winter, their thick hair grows long, to keep them warm in freezing temperatures. Their fur is a light color, so they are camouflaged in the snowy landscape.

◄ Where do ocelots live?

The ocelot is a wild cat that lives in the rainforests of Central and South America. Like many other species of cat, the ocelot is threatened by the destruction of its natural habitat. Ocelots are famous for their beautiful coats. They are reddish-brown in color, with black spots and rosettes. They have a single white spot behind each ear and white markings around the eyes and mouth.

Ocelots can climb, jump, and swim well. They usually find a quiet spot in a tree hollow or crevice to sleep during the day.

Which species of wild cat is the smallest?
The rusty-spotted cat is only 14 in. (35 cm) long and lives in India.

Cats were first tamed over 3,000 years ago, possibly by the ancient Egyptians.

What do caracals hunt?

This agile cat preys on birds, rodents, and small antelopes, stalking a victim before pouncing on it, or knocking low-flying birds out of the air. Caracals sometimes store the remains of their prey in trees or bushes, so they can return to finish it later. Caracals live in dry scrubland in Africa and southwestern Asia.

Lions, Leopards, and Cheetahs

The cat family includes large, wild cats that are commonly known as "big cats". Like their smaller relatives, big cats are meat-eaters, so they must hunt and kill prey to survive. They have keen senses of sight and hearing to help track down their next meal. Some big cats, such as the leopard and snow leopard, like to live alone, but others, such as, the lion and cheetah, live in small groups.

How do lions hunt?

Female lions are called lionesses and they do most of the hunting. They often hunt in pairs, preying on large grassland animals, such as zebra, buffalo, and antelope. Lionesses usually hunt at night and rest during the heat of the day. A group of lions is known as a pride. In a pride, there are several lionesses with their cubs and a few males. The males defend the pride, roaring at intruders to warn them away.

Which mammal is the largest predator in Africa? The lion, which has a shoulder height of up to 4 ft. (1.2 m).

Many big cats, such as the lion, are born with spots, which help to hide them from predators. These spots fade with age.

Do leopards live in groups?

No, leopards are solitary animals. They hunt alone and males only meet with females to reproduce. Leopards live in forests, grasslands, and even deserts in Africa and Asia. Leopards hunt small animals, such as gazelles, pigs, and monkeys, but they are not too fussy, so they will eat birds or insects if food supplies are scarce. Leopards are great climbers and will drag their prey up into the branches of a tree to keep it away from hungry scavengers.

The leopard is the most common of all the big cats and lives in the widest variety of habitats.

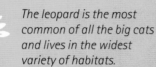

The cheetah is the world's fastest land mammal. It can reach speeds of over 60 mph (100 kmph), but only for about 30 seconds.

Where do cheetahs live?

Cheetahs live in small groups on the vast grassy plains of eastern and southern Africa. They were once common in Asia, as well as in Africa, but were hunted so much that they are now a rare species. Cheetahs hunt by day, because they run after their prey to catch it. They usually hunt small antelope or the young of other grassland animals. When they catch up with their prey, they knock it off balance, then throttle it.

▶ Which is the rarest big cat?

The snow leopard is one of the world's rarest big cats. It lives high up in the mountains of the Himalayas and central Asia. This beautiful animal has been hunted for its thick, winter coat and is now on the brink of extinction. The snow leopard's coat gets thicker during the freezing months of winter. It wraps its long, broad tail around its body for extra warmth.

Big cats roar very loudly but, unlike small cats, they can't purr.

Bears

Bears are the largest meat-eating animals on Earth. There are eight kinds of bear, living in a number of different habitats, including rocky mountains and humid forests. Bears that live in northern parts of the world have thick fur to protect them from the cold. Bears that live in warmer, southern climates do not need to hibernate in winter, as their food supply lasts all year round.

Bears walk with flat feet, so their whole foot touches the ground as they move along.

▼ Can American black bears climb trees?

The American black bear is an excellent climber, using its powerful legs and long claws to grip onto branches and tree trunks. It is also a fast runner, reaching speeds of up to 25 mph (40 kmph) as it chases after prey. However, it mostly feeds on vegetable matter. Despite its name, the American black bear can be dark or reddish-brown as well as black. These colors give the big predator excellent camouflage in the mountainous forests of North America.

◄ What do sloth bears look like?

Sloth bears have long, shaggy black fur, which camouflages them up in the shady trees. They live in the thick, dry forests of India and Sri Lanka. Unfortunately, they are not as common as they once were. Sloth bears are agile climbers, and rest in trees during the day. This makes them look a bit like sloths. However, unlike a true sloth, sloth bears are very active when they are awake and can run faster than humans, if necessary. At night, they spend their waking hours foraging for insects, leaves, and fruits on the forest floor.

Most bears have poor eyesight and hearing, but they make up for this with an excellent sense of smell.

Which bear is grizzly?

he brown bear is the most adaptable
ecies of bear, and is found in Europe and
uthwestern Asia, and across northern Asia to
pan. It also makes its home in mountainous
eas of North America, where it is known as
e grizzly bear. The brown bear is a skilled
nter, and will eat almost anything. In its
tural environment, the brown bear is at the
p of the food chain, and its only enemy is
mans. Brown bears have long been hunted
r their fur and, for this reason, they are
w only found in remote, hilly places.

*Grizzly bears like eating fish.
Sometimes a grizzly bear will wait by a
rushing river to catch a leaping salmon.*

How do bears survive the freezing cold winter months?
Bears that live in cold places make a den in a cave,
then hibernate all winter until the next spring.

*Spectacled bears live
in a warm climate, so
they do not hibernate
in the winters.*

Do spectacled bears wear glasses?

No, but they look like they do. The spectacled
bear is mainly black, but it has a cream-colored
snout and pale rings around its eyes that look
like glasses. The spectacled bear hunts at night,
and sleeps during the day under tree roots or in
rocky caves. The spectacled bear is the only type
of bear to live in South America. It is found
in several different habitats, ranging from
open grassland to humid forest or high
mountain slopes.

Pandas and Raccoons

There are two species of panda. The giant panda is a relative of the bear family. The smaller red panda is more closely related to the raccoon family. Raccoons are very common and familiar animals of North and South America. Most raccoons live in forests, but some have settled in towns and cities, and are considered pests.

The name "raccoon" comes from a Native American word that means "scratches with hands".

▲ What do raccoons eat?

Raccoons are omnivores, and will eat almost anything, for example, fruit, eggs, insects, fish, frogs, and clams. They have nimble front paws, with long fingers that can crack open tough shells. In the wild, raccoons prefer to live in woods, near rivers. They are excellent swimmers and climbers, and are usually more active in the evening. Most male raccoons live alone, only coming together with females to breed. Female raccoons have litters of four or five babies.

Like other bears, the giant panda has poor eyesight, and uses its sense of smell to find food. Bamboo has little nutritional value, and pandas have to eat a lot to stop themselves from starving to death.

Why are giant pandas fussy?

Giant pandas are very fussy eaters, preferring to eat a special type of bamboo that grows in the forests of western China. They need to eat huge amounts of bamboo, and spend at least 16 hours per day feeding. Giant pandas are one of the most distinctive animals in the world, with their thick coats of black and white fur. Female giant pandas have one or two cubs at a time, weighing only about 4 oz. (100 g) each at birth. The tiny cubs grow quickly, and begin to crawl when they are about 10 weeks old.

Where do red pandas live?

Red pandas live in remote mountain forests in the Himalayas, from Nepal to China. Red pandas and giant pandas never meet. Red pandas have a much more varied diet than the giant panda, feeding on a range of roots, bamboo, acorns and fruits. Unlike the giant pandas, red pandas sleep during the day and feed at night. They are very good at climbing trees to find their food.

 Red pandas have sharp claws and short legs, so are well suited for climbing trees.

How many giant pandas are left in the wild?
There are only about 1,000 giant pandas left in the wild.

▼ Do coatimundis eat crabs?

 Coatimundis belong to the same family as red pandas and raccoons. Although the adults have few predators, their young may be attacked by snakes.

Yes, coatimundis of Central and South America do, but they eat other things, too. They can manipulate small prey in their hands, and will sometimes wash food in a river before eating it. Like other raccoons, baby coatimundis are blind and helpless at birth. They feed on their mother's milk for up to four months. Young coatimundis leave the nest when they are about eight months old.

Dogs and Foxes

The domestic dog is a very popular pet, and there are over 100 different breeds. But all these pet dogs have just one common ancestor, known as the wolf. Wolves are one kind of wild dog, and there are 34 other kinds, including foxes, jackals, and dingoes. All wild dogs are carnivores, and are intelligent hunting animals.

Wolves are the largest kind of wild dog. Their sharp fangs and eerie howl sound scary, but wolves rarely attack people.

The desert wolf lives in hot, dry parts of Mexico, Iran and Arabia. It creeps up on its prey as the desert heat means it cannot run for a long chase.

▼ Do jackals hunt in packs?

Jackals usually hunt alone or in pairs. They feed on birds, insects, rodents and lizards, but also prey on bigger animals, such as antelope. Sometimes, jackals will get together in larger groups to share the leftovers of a lion's kill. Jackals are found in Africa, Asia and southeast Europe, where the climate is warm and dry. They live in areas of grassland, where their tawny coat makes them hard to spot. Jackals are often regarded as pests, and people hunt them.

▲ How many wolves in a pack?

Wolves live in family groups. There are usually about 20 wolves in each pack, and at the center is a male and female couple who stay together for life. Their cubs are looked after by all the members of the pack. Hunting in packs is a very good way of tracking down and killing large prey. Gray wolves will hunt animals that are much bigger than themselves, for example, reindeer and musk oxen. They chase their prey until it is exhausted, then move in for the kill.

What are dingoes?

Dingoes are wild dogs that live in the Australian outback. They can survive for long periods on very little water, as they get most of the liquid they need from their food. Dingoes have a varied diet, including lizards, birds, rabbits, and wallabies. They also attack sheep, and are considered a pest by farmers. Dingoes are descended from domestic dogs, and may have been introduced to Australia by the aboriginal people 5,000-8,000 years ago.

When were the first dogs tamed?

The first wild dogs were tamed around 12,000 years ago. Pet dogs have played an important part in people's lives for about 5,000 years.

The red fox is found in more countries than any other meat-eating animal.

Where do red foxes live?

The red fox lives in woodland, and is found in many countries all around the world. It is an omnivore that eats small animals, insects, and fruit. It is also a scavenger, and has moved into towns, and cities, where it forages through garbage cans for food. Foxes are wild dogs, with excellent hearing, keen vision, and a good sense of smell. There are 21 kinds of fox, including the Arctic fox of the far north and the fennec fox of the African and Arabian deserts.

Weasels, Badgers, and Skunks

Weasels, badgers, and skunks look very different from each other, but in fact they are all members of the same large group of mammals, the weasel family. There are 65 species in this family, including nine kinds of skunk and nine kinds of badger. There are many different weasel-like animals, such as stoats, ferrets, martens, and minks. Members of the weasel family are found in every continent except Australia.

Some species of weasel are so small, they can chase prey, such as mice or voles, down their very narrow tunnels.

Skunks spray their attackers from as far away as 13 ft. (4 m). The strong smell lingers for days afterwards.

▲ What do weasels eat?

The European common weasel is a fierce hunter, mainly preying on small mammals such as rabbits, rats, mice, and voles. They have long, slender bodies and can chase their prey along burrows. They can even make a U-turn in the tunnel if necessary, to make a quick exit. Weasels often hunt by day, and have excellent senses of hearing and sight, as well as smell. Young weasels live with their mother, sometimes for a while after they have stopped drinking her milk. They learn how to hunt, and small family groups are sometimes spotted hunting together.

◄ Why are skunks so smelly?

Skunks use their strong smell as a form of self-defense. If a skunk is threatened, it will lift up its tail and squirt out two jets of stinking liquid from a hidden gland. The smell is so bad, it forces the predator to retreat. Skunks live in woods and grassland in North and South America. The most common species of skunk in North America is the striped skunk, but other species include the hog-nosed and spotted skunks. Skunks are small animals, no bigger than a domestic cat.

Where do badgers make their homes?

European badgers live underground in a system of burrows called a sett. They dig the ground with long claws, which they keep sharp by scratching at trees. Badgers are nocturnal animals, eating all kinds of food, but mainly slugs and worms. Badgers have distinctive black and white stripes running down their faces and necks. In the dark, these stripes look like shadows, camouflaging a badger when it is out at night. Its long body is perfect for moving through tunnels.

 A badger's sense of smell is much more powerful than a human's. In fact, it is 700 times stronger. Badgers use this super sense to help them hunt.

What is the smallest carnivore in the world?
The American least weasel. It weighs the same as 10 sugar lumps.

Can minks swim?

he mink is an expert swimmer,
th partially webbed feet that are
ecially adapted for speed in the water.
inks live in burrows that they dig into
e banks of rivers and lakes. They hunt
variety of water creatures, including
ater voles and freshwater fish.
inks have very thick fur, which
eps them warm in cold water.

Baleen Whales

Whales are huge mammals that swim in all the world's oceans. There are two main kinds of whale, toothed whales and baleen whales. The biggest, and most famous species are baleen whales, such as the blue, gray, humpback, and right whales. Despite their massive size, baleen whales feed on the smallest creatures in the oceans, tiny, shrimp-like krill.

Most baleen whales only have one calf every other year. Calves are born in warm seas, because they don't have much fat or blubber to keep them warm.

▼ How do gray whales catch their food?

Gray whales eat similar food to all other baleen whales. Baleen whales feed on krill, which they sift out of the water using huge, comb-like plates. The gray whale migrates vast distances to find the perfect conditions for breeding. It spends the summer in the Arctic Ocean but, when winter comes, it swims thousands of miles south to the warmer waters of the Pacific Ocean, near California. Here, the female gray whale gives birth to her precious calf. Mother and offspring then swim all the way back to the Arctic Ocean.

The biggest threat to whales is hunting by humans. Many species are now endangered.

▲ How does the right whale breathe?

Like all whales, the right whale must swim up to the surface of the water to breathe. It blows air in and out of its lungs through a hole on its back, called a blowhole. The warm air from the whale mixes with the cold ocean air, forming water droplets. This makes it look like the whale is blowing out water. Right whales, and all other species of whale, have to rest sometimes. They do this at the surface of the water, with their tails hanging down, known as "logging".

The humpback whale has the freedom of the sea, and can be found swimming in each of the world's five major oceans.

How do humpback whales attract a mate?

Humpback whales can be acrobatic, considering their huge size. During the breeding season, they are often seen to leap out of the water. Male and female humpbacks sometimes hold each other tight with their long flippers. Whales can communicate underwater. The male humpback whale has its own special song, which lasts for about 35 minutes.

Which is the biggest animal in the world?
The blue whale is the largest animal that ever lived.

▶ Are blue whales born underwater?

Like all other species of whale, blue whales are born underwater, coming out tail first so they don't drown in the first moments of life. Blue whale calves grow very quickly, doubling their weight in their first week. Blue whales are mammals, so their calves drink their mother's milk when they are young. Newborn calves quickly learn to dive down to suckle, swimming up to the surface to breathe afterwards.

A blue whale can live for as long as 80 years.

Dolphins and Porpoises

Dolphins and porpoises are in the cetacean group of mammals. They are toothed whales, with sharp, pointed teeth to help them catch and kill their prey. Most species of dolphin are smaller than their whale relatives, and porpoises are even smaller than dolphins. Porpoises and dolphins have slender, streamlined bodies, which glide quickly through the waves. Fins stand up on their backs to keep them upright in the water.

▼ Are dolphins intelligent?

Dolphins are thought to be some of the most intelligent animals on Earth. A bottle-nosed dolphin's brain is actually larger than a human's. Like all species of dolphin, the bottle-nosed dolphin lives in family groups, known as schools, sometimes of over 100 individuals. Bottle-nosed dolphins are playful animals, and are often seen leaping out of the water. They swim in shallow waters in both the northern and southern oceans.

▼ What do porpoises look like?

The common porpoise looks like a small dolphin, but it has a short snout and a small, cone-shaped head. It usually lives in pairs or small groups, and is not as playful as its fun-loving dolphin relatives. The common porpoise is not as common as it once was. It is in danger because it has been hunted so much for its meat and oil.

Like all whales, dolphins and porpoises breathe through a blowhole on the top of their head. They must come up to the surface of the water to breathe.

Most species of dolphin have about 200 small, sharp teeth in their long, beak-shaped snouts. The teeth are perfectly designed for catching and holding onto prey.

▶ Which dolphins are the best acrobats?

Spinner dolphins are named after the acrobatic, spinning twists that they perform when they leap out of the sea. Spinner dolphins are most active after a rest, and do their most amazing jumps at night. They are sociable animals, and will mix with other ocean species, such as the spotted dolphin. All dolphins make clicking sounds, which travel through the water and bounce back when they hit nearby objects. This helps the dolphin to track down prey, and to know when there are predators nearby. Dolphins have a sense organ called a "melon" on their foreheads, which helps them detect the size and position of other sea creatures.

 Bottle-nosed dolphins migrate to find warmer waters to breed in. As they do so, they lose weight, so they do not overheat. When they return to cooler waters, they put weight back on to keep them warm.

Which dolphin is the biggest? The killer whale is the biggest member of the dolphin family.

Killer whales have very large appetites. A killer whale from the Bering Sea was found with 32 seals in its stomach.

How big is a killer whale?

The killer whale grows up to 33 ft. (10 m) long, which is about the length of three cars. It is a fearsome predator and will sometimes hunt in packs to kill animals larger than itself, such as bigger species of whale. The killer whale has a very varied diet, and will eat fish, squid, seals, and even birds. Killer whales live in all the world's oceans, mainly close to the coastline. Sometimes they swim onto the shore to snatch a seal, then let the waves wash them back out again.

Seals, Sea Lions, and Walruses

Seals, sea lions, and walruses are all sea mammals, which means that they breathe air, even though they spend most of their time in the water. There are 34 different species of seal, sea lion, and walrus. They give birth to their young on land, quickly returning to the oceans to hunt for food. Baby seals, sea lions, and walruses all drink their mother's milk after they are born.

Seals can dive underwater for up to half an hour at a time. Their heartbeat slows down to about 15 beats a minute, so they do not use up much oxygen.

▼ Do elephant seals have trunks?

Elephant seals are named after the males' long, floppy snouts, which look a bit like elephant trunks. Like the elephant, the elephant seal is very big and has thick, wrinkled skin. Male elephant seals are almost twice the size of females. Living in the frozen waters of the Arctic and Antarctic, elephant seals need a thick layer of blubber under their skin to keep them warm. Elephant seals spend up to 90 percent of their time under water, only coming to the surface to breathe and take short rests.

Elephant seals can make loud sounds through their long, inflatable snouts. During the breeding season, males will challenge each other to a fight with noisy calls.

Why are sea lions' flippers like oars?

Sea lions use their big front flippers like oars, to propel themselves through the water. A sea lion can swim as fast as 25 mph (40 kmph). Sea lions also use their front flippers to support their bulky bodies as they sit upright on rocks. Unlike seals, they can waddle along on land, again with the help of their flexible front flippers.

◀ How do gray seals find their food?

Gray seals have long whiskers, which are so sensitive they detect changes in the water as shoals of tasty fish swim past. This helps gray seals detect and follow their prey. Gray seals eat many different kinds of fish. They bring larger ones to the surface, where they grip them in their front flippers and bite off their heads.

Gray seals give birth to their young on isolated beaches. The young, called pups, are born covered in creamy white fur, which they shed after about three weeks.

Which seal is the heaviest? The elephant seal is the biggest and heaviest seal. The male weighs almost as much as an Asian elephant.

Why do walruses have tusks?

The tusks of a walrus are actually long canine teeth. Walruses use their tusks to poke around on the seabed, digging up clams and other shellfish to eat. Walrus tusks are also useful for boring holes in the ice, and for helping a walrus to lift itself out of the water for a rest. Walruses live in the freezing waters of the Arctic Ocean. They have tough skin, which is about 1 in. (2.5 cm) thick, and underneath this skin is a layer of fatty blubber to keep them warm.

When walruses lie on rocks to bask in the sun, their skin turns pink. This is because blood is rushing to the surface of their thick skin, to cool their bodies down.

Camels, Llamas, and Alpacas

The camel family includes the large, desert-dwelling camels of Africa and Asia, and also the smaller, mountain-climbing llamas and alpacas of South America. All members of the camel family are excellent at adapting to very hostile environments. They all have unusually long necks, and their eyes, ears and nostrils are set high up on their heads, so they can spot a threat when it is still a long way off.

The dromedary camel can go for an amazing 10 months without water, if it still has access to grazing. When it finds water again, it can drink nine huge buckets in just 15 minutes.

▼ Do Bactrian camels live in the desert?

Wild Bactrian camels live in the Gobi Desert in northern Asia. Conditions in this environment are extreme, with scorching hot summers and harsh, severe winters. The Bactrian camel is well adapted to this varied climate, with long, shaggy fur that protects it from both the heat and the cold. When strong winds whip up a storm in the desert, it is very important for a Bactrian camel not to breathe in too much sand and dust. To protect itself, it kneels down, presses its ears flat and shuts its eyes and nostrils. Then it simply waits until the storm passes.

▲ How many humps does a dromedary have?

Most camels live in the hot, dry deserts of Arabia and Africa. These camels all have one hump, and are called dromedary camels. They have longer legs, and are not as heavily built as Bactrian camels. Dromedary camels are useful animals. They are hardy, and can survive high temperatures and harsh conditions. They are famous for carrying heavy loads across the desert, but they also provide their owners with milk and meat. Their hides and hair can be used to make clothes, rugs, and tents. Even their droppings can be used as fuel.

Unlike the dromedary, most Bactrian camels are wild, roaming free in their natural desert habitat. Their wide, padded feet stop them from sinking into the soft sand.

Where do llamas live?

llamas live along the Andes mountain range of South America. These strong animals can breathe the thin air ound at very high altitudes. Unlike their camel relatives, amas do not have humps, but they do have long legs and re fast runners. Llamas have shaggy fur, which comes in variety of colors. They are medium-sized animals, about ft. (1.2 m) at shoulder height. That is about as tall as ten-year-old child, but they weigh roughly three imes as much.

Llamas were first tamed for human use over 4,000 years ago. They are used to carry goods in inaccessible mountain areas.

What is inside a camel's hump? A camel's hump is a store of fat, not water. When a camel has to go without food or water, it uses this fat reserve to stay alive.

What do alpacas and camels have in common?

Although the alpaca lives in another continent and looks nothing like a camel, the two animals are members of the same family, the camelids. Alpacas and llamas are so alike that they are sometimes thought to be the same species. They are both descended from the guanaco, which was tamed for human use thousands of years ago, but is still found in the wild today.

Like all members of the camel family, alpacas make sounds to communicate with the rest of the herd, such as low, bleating calls to warn of approaching danger.

Monkeys and Baboons

Monkeys are sociable animals that live in big family groups. There are two main kinds, Old World and New World monkeys. New World monkeys live in South America, and most have gripping tails that help them swing through the trees. Old World monkeys come from Africa and Asia. Many Old World monkeys also live in the treetops, but some, like the baboon, mostly live on the ground.

▼ Are colobus monkeys good climbers?

The colobus monkey is an excellent climber, and hardly ever leaves the trees of the African forest. Its long tail does not grip onto branches, but it helps the monkey keep its balance high up off the ground, and escape from predators such as eagles and chimpanzees. Colobus monkeys live in small groups of up to 15 individuals, with one adult male leader, and three or four females with young. The females are close relatives, and will often care for each other's babies soon after they are born.

Colobus monkeys are very noisy, calling loudly at dawn and dusk to mark out their troop territory. They make roaring, snorting, purring, honking, and screaming sounds.

◄ Why do mandrills have bright faces?

Mandrills are a species of baboon that lives in the rainforests of West Africa. Male mandrills are twice as big as females, and look very impressive. They have bright red noses and bright blue cheeks, which stand out from their dark fur coats. They also have blue and red bottoms. It seems that all of these markings are there to help a male mandrill attract a much less colorful and interesting mate.

Like most monkeys, mandrills rely heavily on visual or vocal communication to understand each other. Mandrills use a variety of sounds to express themselves.

Why do ring-tailed lemurs have long tails?

Lemurs communicate with each other using their tails. In tall grass, they point their tails upwards, so the rest of their group can see them.

Baboons spend a lot of time grooming and cleaning each other. This helps them to form bonds in the group, especially between mothers and babies.

Are lemurs monkeys?

Lemurs are primates, which is a large group of animals that includes apes and monkeys. However, lemurs are not actually monkeys, even though they look and behave like members of that animal family. Lemurs live in forests on the island of Madagascar, off the coast of Africa. They are not found anywhere else in the world.

How do baboons move?

Baboons live in Africa and the Arabian Peninsula. They are large monkeys that live in open country, moving about on all fours. Although they can climb, baboons spend most of their time on the ground, in family groups called troops. Some troops have over 100 members, always led by one male. Anubis baboons live in troops, protecting them from predators, such as lions. Baboons will also guard their territory to prevent other baboon troops from straying into it. Baboon troops have a strict hierarchy, and males have to fight each other to earn their ranking in the group.

 Most species of lemur live high up in trees, like monkeys. However, the ring-tailed lemur is different, and spends most of its time on the forest floor.

New World Monkeys

New World monkeys live in the forests of Central and South America. All New World monkeys are fantastic climbers, with most species using their strong tails as a third "arm" to help them grip tightly onto branches. There are many different kinds of New World monkey, including the large spider monkey, the howler monkey, and the smaller marmosets and tamarins.

Are monkeys intelligent? Scientists believe monkeys are very intelligent, with large brains for their size, and quick reactions.

▼ How do spider monkeys move?

Spider monkeys have very long arms and legs, and an even longer, stronger tail. They swing through the trees faster than a human can run. They need to move quickly to escape from predators, such as soaring eagles in the skies above, or stealthy jaguars on the forest floor below. Spider monkeys can also hang by their tails, leaving both hands free to eat food, such as leaves and fruit. When spider monkeys rest, they wind the tip of their tails around a branch to stop them falling out of the tree.

Black spider monkeys spend almost half of their time resting, and the remainder is evenly split between eating and moving about to find food.

Golden lion tamarins use their long, thin fingers to pick insects out of the bark. They also eat snails, lizards, fruit, and leaves.

The howler monkey has a specially adapted voice box, which makes it possible to project sound over a huge distance.

How noisy are howler monkeys?

owler monkeys make very loud howling noises to warn other oops not to invade their territory. The male leader of a howler onkey troop is the loudest of all. His booming calls can be heard far as 3 mi. (5 km) away. A troop of red howler monkeys usually s about 10 members, with only one or two males in the group. d howlers live high up in the top canopy of the rainforest, where ey forage for their favorite leaves, fruit and flowers. They rest a t, sometimes sleeping for over 15 hours a day.

 The pygmy marmoset is the smallest species of monkey in the world. Its body is just 5 in. (13 cm) long, which is the size of a hamster. This little monkey's tail is about twice the length of its body.

How big are marmosets?

armosets are very small monkeys that live in the South merican rainforest. They are not much bigger than squirrels. armosets have claws on their hands and feet, not flat nails ke most monkeys. Unlike other New World monkeys, they nnot grip and swing through the branches with their tails. ost species of marmoset eat insects, but they will also eat uit, seeds, sap, and gum from bark, if necessary. A mother armoset will carry her tiny baby on her back while she rages in the trees for food.

Is the golden lion tamarin endangered?

The golden lion tamarin is one of the rarest mammals in the world, with very few left in the wild. They live in the coastal forest of southeast Brazil. Fortunately, golden lion tamarins have been bred successfully in captivity, and can be reintroduced into their natural environment.

Apes

Of all the animals in the world, apes are our closest relatives. Like humans, apes are intelligent mammals, which can walk upright and live for many years. Apes care for their young in family groups, and are very sociable. Apes are very hairy, and have long, strong arms with shorter, weaker legs. They are great climbers, and live in forests. There are four types of ape, chimpanzees, gorillas, orangutans, and gibbons.

Gibbons have long arms which help them swing through the trees.

▲ Which species of gibbon is the biggest?

Gibbons are the smallest kind of ape. The largest species of gibbon is the siamang gibbon, which grows up to 3 ft. (90 cm) tall. That's about as tall as a three-year-old child. Gibbons make up for their small size with speed. They can swing through the trees at speeds of up to 20 mph (32 kmph). That is a fast sprint at ground level. There are nine species of gibbon, all of which are known as "lesser" apes. Gibbons are different from the great apes in that they spend all their time high up in the treetops. They rest sitting upright in the forks of trees.

◄ How big are gorillas?

Gorillas are the biggest kind of ape, growing up to 5.9 ft. (1.75 m) tall. That's about adult human height. There are two main species of gorilla, both found in the forests of central Africa. Gorillas live in family groups, led by a single, large male called a silverback. Baby gorillas are slow developers. They do not walk until they are about ten months old. Young gorillas feed on their mother's milk for about two years, and sleep with their mothers for three years using leafy branches from the forest as bedding.

A troop of gorillas stays in one place until most of the food has been eaten. Then, the troop moves on to a new spot, allowing all the plants to grow back.

What do chimpanzees eat?

Chimpanzees live in the forests of central and western Africa, and have a varied diet. Mostly, they eat fruit, leaves, and seeds, but they also enjoy ants and termites. Sometimes they hunt larger prey, such as bush pigs and small monkeys. Chimpanzees are one of the few mammals to use "tools" to help them eat. A chimpanzee will use a stick to tease termites out of their nest, and crack open nuts with a stone.

Chimpanzees live in groups of between 15 and 80 family members. Older chimpanzees in a troop can be sixty years old.

Which ape pulls faces? All apes pull faces! The chimpanzee has many different expressions, such as playful, irritated, angry, and frightened.

The name "orangutan" comes from the Malay language, and means "man of the forest".

Where do orangutans live?

Orangutans live in the rainforests of Southeast Asia. But now, as so many of these rainforests have been destroyed, orangutans are extremely rare. These beautiful, orange-haired primates are well camouflaged in the dark, dappled shadows of their natural habitat. Like gorillas and chimpanzees, orangutans make a cozy nest to rest in. Orangutans search for food at dawn and dusk, but will rest in their nest at midday, and sleep there at night.

Index